The Big Book of Cats

Photographs: Erich Tylinek   Text: Manfred Bürger

The Big Book of Cats

Line drawings by Michael Lissmann

David & Charles

Newton Abbot London

Translated from the German by Alisa Jaffa

First published in the German Democratic
Republic by Edition Leipzig

First published in the United Kingdom
by David & Charles, Newton Abbot, 1980

ISBN: 0 7153 7836 8

Copyright © 1979 by Edition Leipzig

Produced by Druckerei Fortschritt Erfurt
Printed in the German Democratic Republic

Contents

Ink and brush drawing by Joseph Hegenbarth

T. S. Eliot ## The Naming of Cats

The Naming of Cats is a difficult matter,
*   It isn't just one of your holiday games:*
You may think at first I'm as mad as a hatter
*   When I tell you a cat must have three different names.*
First of all, there's the name that the family use daily,
*   Such as Peter, Augustus, Alonzo or James,*
Such as Victor or Jonathan, George or Bill Bailey;
*   All of them sensible everyday names.*
There are fancier names if you think they sound sweeter,
*   Some for the gentlemen, some for the dames:*
Such as Plato, Admetus, Electra, Demeter—
*   But all of them sensible everyday names.*
But I tell you, a cat needs a name that's particular,
*   A name that's peculiar, and more dignified,*
Else how can he keep up his tail perpendicular,
*   Or spread out his whiskers, or cherish his pride?*
Of names of this kind, I can give you a quorum,
*   Such as Munkustrap, Quaxo or Coricopat,*
Such as Bombalurina, or else Jellylorum—
*   Names that never belong to more than one cat.*
But above and beyond there's still one name left over,
*   And that is the name that you never will guess;*
The name that no human research can discover—
*   But the cat himself knows, and will never confess.*
When you notice a cat in profound meditation,
*   The reason, I tell you, is always the same:*
His mind is engaged in a rapt contemplation
*   Of the thought, of the thought, of the thought of his name:*
*   His ineffable effable*
*   Effanineffable*
Deep and inscrutable singular Name.

Choosing and caring for a cat

The problem of choice

A pet animal can enrich the life of its owner in a great many ways, bringing interest and companionship and, in a surprising number of cases, giving purpose and support where life may have seemed to have lost its meaning. Of all the domestic animals one might choose there is none, except perhaps for certain breeds of dogs and horses, which can aesthetically match the cat. The beauty of its body structure, which is almost unchanged from that of the wild species from which it evolved, the lustre and softness of its fur, its colouring, elegance, litheness and sure-footedness, its flattering, yet distinctly independent nature, make the cat an ideal domestic pet for many.

However, the engaging playfulness of a young kitten should not be allowed to entice you into taking on a cat, without first reflecting on how to handle such a house companion. Are you really a cat lover? For that you must be if you are properly to keep and care for a cat. Before acquiring a pet of any kind it is important to consider what sort of animal would suit you best, and to compare the merits of cat and dog, rabbit and tortoise, tropical fish or horse or whatever other creature takes your fancy.

Ask yourself a number of important questions: 'What do I expect from this would-be house companion? How do I mean to keep it? Shall I be able to devote sufficient time to the animal? Am I prepared to muster the energy necessary daily to care for the animal and train it? Can I provide it with a suitable environment?'

In most cases it is not enough to want to provide the kitten with 'a beautiful life'; from the outset it is essential to realise that a cat normally has a life-span of only 12–15 years (though cats have been known, exceptionally, to live as long as 20 years, and even longer). You must be ready to care for it throughout its life and prepared for the sad day, which inevitably will come, when you have to take leave of your faithful pet.

In the following pages we shall set out the essential details of routine daily care, how to overcome training problems, possible complications in illness, and many other eventualities, some of them negative. Readiness to accept the negative aspects of a domestic animal and house companion is a measure of one's love for animals, which demands a spirit of sacrifice, and a sense of responsibility. However, it cannot be stressed too often: the love of an animal—which is an implicit understanding of the nature and uniqueness of every animal—is not demonstrated by attempts to turn it into a human being.

Cat or dog? Deciding on a cat or dog involves essentially different considerations. These two domestic pets have completely different natural life styles. As a descendant of the wolf, the dog seeks a genuine attachment and wants to fit in, in a way akin to its antecedent's subordination to the hierarchy of the wolfpack. In the majority of cases, the dog needs a task; the goal in training most breeds was and remains directed towards achievable objectives, whether of watching, guarding, hunting, sniffing out scent, ratting, etc. Dogs require a great deal of exercise, movement and occupation in the company of

8

their master. The cat on the other hand is predominantly a solitary animal, and does not seek subordination, for the most part loving peace and calm, and being petted and stroked—but only when it feels like it. A cat in the house tends to create an atmosphere of calm and well-being around itself, which transmits itself in a beneficial way to the people it lives with.

Mongrel or pedigree? Having decided on a cat, for whatever reasons, now comes the question of whether the cat should be a purebreed, i.e. have a pedigree, or whether to opt for an ordinary mongrel moggie. The choice should never be made on the basis of how much money is available. One's choice may perhaps be influenced by having seen some particularly beautiful creature at a show or in a cattery, or by the desire to go in for breeding. A pedigree is merely a certificate showing parentage. You could produce a pedigree for a mongrel cat but a pedigree is usually a proof of forebears which conform in colour, variety and type and show the cat to be purebred—and nowadays the term pedigree has taken the place of 'purebreed' in general usage.

As nowadays domestic cats are seldom kept as working animals to catch mice and rats—at any rate, in towns—its hunting prowess is unlikely to be a relevant consideration affecting the choice of cat. Nevertheless, given the opportunity, 75 per cent of all house cats are mouse-catchers but among pedigree cats the long-haired varieties seem to be less interested or accomplished as mousers. Another fundamental difference is in the temperament of the cats. Long-haired cats are often considerably quieter, even phlegmatic, compared with short-haired cats. Orientals usually want considerable attention from and involvement with their humans, whilst long-haired cats require a great deal more grooming care, the fur requiring daily attention.

Certain breeds are often described as 'gentle and withdrawn', 'very shy', 'very affectionate', 'requiring lots of love' and so on, but in my view such characteristics are not necessarily associated with particular breeds, as cats tend to be highly individual and vary from one to another.

If you have decided on a pedigree cat, then the Governing Council of the Cat Fancy will supply a list of breeders of particular varieties. A good breeder will not usually part with a kitten under ten weeks old, and will already have had it inoculated against Feline Infectious Enteritis. If a certificate of inoculation is not provided with the cat you should arrange for this to be done immediately. With any new cat a veterinary check-up is always a good idea.

When buying a pedigree cat, make certain that you obtain an application for registration or, in the case of a cat already registered, a transfer form, which, in both cases, should be signed by the breeder. If you have a cat as a kitten you will be able to guide its training and enjoy the very positive experience of watching the kitten develop and mature into a young cat.

Make sure that it is healthy and without deformity. It should be lively and playful, have a smooth, glossy coat, pink membranes and bright clear eyes. With an older cat the adjustment to a new environment and retraining may be difficult if it has habits that you wish to change but an older cat may suit some people who would find the havoc which a kitten can wreak all too disruptive.

9

If you are acquiring a new cat the question of which sex to have arises immediately. Tom or female—both have their advantages and disadvantages. Their vigorous sexual urges cannot be repressed and when a female is on heat she cannot be held in the house, or males prevented from trying to reach her, unless all doors, windows and other apertures are kept closed. The almost nightly 'concerts' of caterwauling can be a severe test of nerves. It is usually the owner of the female who suffers most, since she remains in the vicinity of the house, while the toms from the entire neighbourhood converge upon her. The owner of the female also has to cope with the results and becomes responsible for putting down at birth those of the litter which cannot be accommodated. (See chapter on sexual life and reproduction, section unwanted offspring.) Yet there are many cat-lovers who would not miss the experience of the birth and raising of a litter of kittens. When a female is on heat the tom cat will spray strong, unpleasant-smelling urine around the house, making himself extremely unpopular, and will mark his home territory in this way right through the year. The only tom worth keeping as a stud is a purebreed. It should be kept in a stud enclosure, to which visiting females (queens) may be brought.

If a tom is to be kept in an apartment, neutering is really the only course open to the owner and a responsible owner will neuter any tom not being kept deliberately for stud. If this were more commonly done the misery of unwanted and abandoned kittens might gradually disappear. As a result the domestic cat might become something of a rarity, and accordingly be more valued and appreciated. A neutered cat becomes more affectionate and will roam less. Given sufficient opportunity for exercise, which can also be provided by playing with the animal, the neutered tom need by no means become fat, lethargic and lazy. If the young tom is neutered early enough, its sexual instinct will be destroyed. If alteration is left until after puberty, the tom's sexual drive will gradually abate. A female can also be sterilised by an operation, or spayed, removing its ovaries. It is difficult to keep sexually mature cats shut indoors while they are on heat. The queen (female) will become increasingly over-stimulated, which will result in her heat periods occurring in more and more rapid succession. This can produce a change in the temperament of the animal, making her difficult and aggressive and even unclean. It may also lead to serious medical problems. Sterilisation of the tom or queen will in no way adversely affect the characteristics that endear them to us. There may be a slightly higher incidence of some geriatric skin conditions and other problems of hormone balance but they can be treated and these cats would probably have suffered from them anyway. They are negligible compared with the other problems avoided.

The sex of young kittens is plainly visible for only two to three days after birth. If the evidence is missed at that time it may be some weeks or months before the novice can be absolutely certain of a kitten's gender. The easiest guide is the distance between the anal opening and the genitals, which is greater in a tom than in a female, while the anal opening lies closer to the tail of the tom.

Having acquired a young kitten, its owner is quite likely to find the first few days a fairly noisy business, depending on its temperament. The kitten may try to call its absent mother and siblings by miaowing pitifully. However, this will very soon stop. In the first few hours the animal should not be handled, but just observed. A cat needs considerably longer than a dog to adjust to changed circumstances. Step by step it takes possession of its new surroundings. In a large apartment, it should first be allowed to explore one room thoroughly before being introduced to the remaining rooms. Only then should you play with it, and encourage it to race about. A ball, such as a ping-pong ball, which is neither so small that it can be swallowed, nor so big as to make it awkward to play with, is an ideal toy. But even a screw of paper dangling from a length of string will entice the cat to lively play. The string should not, however, be left for the cat to play with, as it can get itself tangled up or even be strangled while playing. Plenty of attention lavished on the kitten at this stage will soon make it forget its earlier playfellows.

If there are already other animals in the house the new arrival can first be put for a short time in a secure pen and the established family pet allowed into the same room, so that the two can sniff at each other undisturbed. With an older cat a kitten can be rubbed with a little of the used litter from the litter tray to transfer the smell of the older cat to its fur and aid the kitten's acceptance.

Apart from a suitable healthy diet, ample fresh air and sunshine are the best ways to make the kitten thrive. Every available opportunity should be used to the full, particularly for animals restricted by urban flat-life. A balcony, a safe window ledge, or even a place on the floor that catches the sun through an open window can provide beneficial doses of the sunshine they enjoy. Damp and draughts should be avoided. But although kittens adore warmth above all else, they should not be unduly coddled, as this can be detrimental to their health.

The attachment of a cat to its owner becomes evident if there is a sudden separation, such as, for example, if the animal has to be hospitalised, or if the owner is unavoidably absent. On the return of the cat, or its owner, the animal will not stir from its owner's feet. Moving house or even spending the night away from its own home can make the cat very nervous and unsettled. Provided the owner is close at hand, however, and reassures the cat with redoubled care and attention, it will soon display curiosity about its new surroundings and begin, albeit cautiously, to explore. From then on, it should settle back to its normal way of life. The young kitten should not be allowed out in the garden or the neighbourhood too soon. Not until the tie to its owner has been firmly established should this be attempted. If the cat is used to being attached to a lead, the first exploratory walks in the garden should be taken together. The settling-in of the kitten will undeniably be facilitated if, right from the start, a regular daily routine is adopted with a set time for feeding, grooming, play and resting, etc. By this means the cat's 'internal clock' will quickly and surely establish itself.

Why have a cat? A cat lover once put it very aptly and succinctly: 'Cats are enchanting house companions, good friends and splendidly entertaining.' A cat often means a great deal to older people in particular.

To combat the frequent loneliness and enjoy a happy old age, it is essential to have a purpose in one's later years. All too often solitary people describe a cat as the 'sunshine of their old age'. For many people the cat provides physical contact, for the cat is an animal that loves being stroked and petted. Once its affection has been won, a cat can enrich the life of a human being and make it far more interesting, while it can also protect its owner from developing psychological problems.

Animals have a profound effect on the development of children's characters. Living with them gradually promotes a sense of responsibility and consideration for animals, which in turn leads to consideration for other people. Many children, who do not come into contact with animals early enough or have them to care for and look after, develop an attitute towards them as a result of which they retain a life-long fear of animals.

Mouse- and rat-catching used to be the reason for keeping cats, but nowadays they are primarily kept as pets, except on the land and in institutions, factories and large store places. Often this task has been superseded by the use of chemical agents (which may sometimes endanger the cats themselves).

The genuine friendship that can develop between different animals never ceases to affect the owner afresh each time as a very special experience. There are many examples involving cats. The innumerable cases of friendship between dog and cat will be related in detail later in this book. Even friendships between cats and a great variety of birds are by no means uncommon. All this is simply a matter of habit, and the right training—there is nothing unnatural about it. In the Magdeburg Zoo, there is nearly always a cat in the breeding section, which will from time to time take over as a wet-nurse for raising other breeds. She is on such trusting terms with all the different birds that are kept there, that they quite literally hop about on her head. Cats have even been known to foster mice and rats, while continuing to hunt mice and rats living wild—this, too, is not unusual. There are known cases of cats having reared martens, squirrels, skunks, hedgehogs and many other animals.

The question of a cat's attachment to a human remains essentially something of a mystery. It is more a matter of the individual relationship between the cat and its owner. Very carefully raised cats that live in constant close contact with their owner understandably become thoroughly trusting, and develop a much closer and affectionate relationship. This is even more marked in the case of pedigree cats, which require far more attention than ordinary house cats. The cat expresses its deep attachment to its owner through a variety of particular actions, such as by giving mating sounds or certain cries usually directed towards its young. Cats that do not have such a firm attachment usually have a more pronounced home or territorial fixation. For these cats the house and territory are decisive, while the owner comes second. Such cats adhere firmly to one place, and to move them to a new home is a much more difficult and complicated undertaking than with owner-fixated cats.

As a rule, cats do not like being accompanied on walks. Unlike dogs, they will usually stop at their 'territorial frontier' and sit there waiting for the return of their owner. Their 'homing instinct', too, is usually inferior to that of a dog.

Whereas, as mentioned earlier, the importance of cats as mousers and ratters has diminished considerably—at any rate in urban areas—it is nevertheless worth noting the findings of studies which show what cats eat when left to fend for themselves. These were

The cat as a useful house pet

frequently cats that had been wantonly abandoned and had become semi- or entirely feral. The customary disparagement of cats as 'bird-killers' appears a trifle absurd in the light of the following statistics. Is the cat really such a great enemy of birdlife and small game? Various investigations undertaken by one university institute yielded the following findings: the stomachs of more than 60 semi-feral cats were found to contain 93.8 per cent voles, and 6.2 per cent mice, field-mice and harvest-mice. In only three cases were the remains of small birds found, and likewise in three cases, squirrel remains. In two instances there were fish remains, which came from kitchen refuse. Only 49 per cent contained any wild prey at all, about 30 per cent contained some domestic food. The stomach contents of 171 cats consisted predominantly of rodent remains, i.e. 89.1 per cent; 4.4 per cent contained bird remains, while 3.8 per cent contained insects, and 2.1 per cent worms and snails.

There have been and still are numerous examples of cats being most successfully employed, as it were—and budgeted for—by city and government bodies, port authorities, on ships, in businesses, etc. It has been estimated that approximately ten tons of grain are saved from destruction by keeping one mouse-catching cat. The contribution of the cat towards health maintenance came to be appreciated amidst the rubble of ruined European cities at the end of World War II.

| The cat's predatory instinct | Prof. Paul Leyhausen, the German scientist, is the leading researcher into the behaviour of cats in hunting and devouring prey and what follows is known from his work.

All cats engage in stalking and hunting. They will either prowl through their hunting territory, or they will lie in wait at mouse-holes or haunts known to them, and at other places regularly visited by other forms of prey. Once the cat has spotted a likely prey, it will slink along, very close to the ground, waiting until it is within a few metres of its prey before adopting an ambush position. The whole length of the body is then extended flat on the ground, with the tip of the tail twitching slightly, the head craned forwards, the whiskers splayed outwards and the ears pricked forwards. As if in slow motion, the cat prepares to spring. The rear paws are slowly pushed backwards, while the cat continues to fix the prey with its eyes. Finally, as if shot from a bow, in two or three mighty bounds, the cat leaps at its prey. As a rule it does not approach so close to its prey that it can reach it in one single leap. If it misses its victim, it will not chase it far, and sometimes not at all. Even when it is ambushing from above, the cat will not spring straight down on to its prey, but will first land securely on the ground very close by, in order to have its claws available for immediate attack. The advantages of this behaviour are steadiness, an immediate means of defence, and better control of its jump. A cat catches crawling insects, by attacking with both paws simultaneously. Flying insects may be knocked down with a paw or caught in the mouth. Birds hopping along on the ground will be watched and sighted for some time. Meanwhile the hopping bird is constantly shifting its position so that the cat follows it and lies in wait again—but before it is ready to pounce, the bird is usually up and away. The cat's behaviour when lying in wait is clearly aimed specifically at catching small rodents. The prolonged waiting period, during which the exact distance is assessed, is aimed at preventing the mouse or rat from escaping back down its hole.

13

A smaller creature is seized immediately by the cat in its sharp teeth, though sometimes it will place one or both front paws on it. It is primarily the movement of the prey, and to a lesser extent its shape and size, that make the cat drop its pouncing hold. Speed and direction play an important part in this. Only if the prey moves away from or across the cat's path, is the cat prompted to chase and catch it. A prey that moves towards the cat, however, puts the cat on the defensive, and may even make it retreat.

The inborn predatory instinct must be developed by experience, which teaches the cat to recognise the prey even when it is standing quite still, and to distinguish between different kinds of prey, and also enables the cat to react merely to the sound or the scent of the prey. Inexperienced young cats will not attack immobile prey.

The cat bites the neck of its prey, usually sinking its canine teeth into the spinal cord, which causes instant death. If the prey does not die immediately and tries to defend itself, the cat holds fast with its teeth and cuffs it swiftly with its claws. In the case of larger creatures, the cat will roll on to its back, still holding on to its prey, and work on it with powerful blows from its back paws. This physical coordination can be elicited in any young kitten at play, by turning it on its back and trying to hold it down with one's hand.

Fish are caught very neatly by the cat, which scoops them out of the water with one front paw. This is why fish tanks should always be kept covered!

The whiskers fill an important function in the cat's seizure of its prey. As the cat pounces, they are fully extended, and from then on cover the prey, so that the cat can sense the slightest movement of its catch. The whiskers can also transmit information as to the position of the head, rear and tail of the creature in the cat's grasp.

All the movements involved in catching prey may sometimes be carried out with a substitute object, or even without anything at all. Every kind of individual action involved in the catching of prey, except for the death-dealing 'bite', is acted out in play.

After the catch   It is rare for the cat to start eating its catch immediately at the spot where it was caught. After putting it down the cat will usually conduct a curious 'walkabout', investigating the immediate surroundings with the utmost care, even if they are entirely familiar to it. This is presumably to give the cat time to wind down from the tension of the kill.

14

Birds the size of a blackbird are plucked by the cat, whereas it will devour smaller birds complete with feathers. Mammals, if their fur is longer than 10 mm ($\frac{4}{10}$ in) are also skinned. The cat spits out the feathers and fur, removing them by jerking its head to and fro. In between, it will lick its own fur in order to free its tongue from any down that has stuck to it.

The cat almost always starts by eating the head of its catch. Among several hundred instances observed by Prof. Leyhausen there were only three exceptions. It seems to prefer to eat in a squatting position, although it will also do so standing up. As a rule, the cat does not chew, but uses its fangs to cut up its prey into chunks or strips, which are then swallowed whole.

In principle, cats can catch any living creature of their own size or smaller. Prof. Leyhausen observed that they generally do not attempt to attack creatures larger than rats or pigeons. Insects, from houseflies to ladybirds, are eagerly chased and usually greedily eaten, too. Fish, frogs, lizards and snakes are killed and frequently also consumed. Shrews and moles are caught, but have never been recorded as being eaten. Young wild rabbits, squirrels, polecats and weasels are occasionally caught. However the favourite prey are rats and mice. The intensity with which the cat chases after rats does not depend on the size or the strength of the cat, but is more a matter of temperament, and undoubtedly also depends on how experienced the cat is in fighting. A fully-grown rat can successfully defend itself against a cat and sometimes even put it to flight.

Hunting technique gradually develops of its own accord in the kitten, quite independently of any experience. At about three weeks, the kitten begins to examine every object around it, both living and inanimate, by tentatively pawing it. In intermittent stages, it goes through all the transitions until it will suddenly grab an object with extended claws, and drag it towards itself. When playing, the cat paws with its claws retracted, often turning its head to one side, and occasionally using its teeth as well.

When her kittens are about four weeks old, a free-ranging mother cat will bring her catch back to the nest, where she will devour it herself, frequently growling. In the weeks that follow she will begin to give the kittens a share of the catch. Leyhausen maintains that the mother cat is not teaching the kittens but, by letting the prey go, she prompts their hunting instincts. The mother's swift recapture of the prey compels the kittens to try to be swifter still. It is simply a matter of increasing the stimuli by competition until the prey is killed and devoured. When the catch is a smaller creature, for example a mouse, a mock capture is often enacted, the last ingredient of which, namely, the killing, appears restrained.

The best way to keep a cat is to offer it the freedom of choice between being indoors or outdoors. However, if you live in an apartment, in a town, or by a main road this may be too difficult or too dangerous. If your cats are not neutered and you want to breed there are really only two alternatives—either to keep them in a firmly shut room or preferably, in an outdoor pen. Otherwise, unplanned breeding is a continual risk.

For pedigree breeding a pen with several compartments is essential. This must contain heated indoor chambers with corresponding outdoor areas which the cat can enter and leave, preferably at will. For a stud tom, the accommodation must include extra rooms with an outdoor pen for visiting queens. When furnishing an outdoor pen, in addition to providing a litter tray and food and water dishes, remember to include scratching and climbing posts, and perches. The floor should consist of half sand or gravel, and half grass or, failing all else, concrete. The wire mesh used for the cage should be as narrow a gauge as possible, to prevent a young kitten poking its head through in the course of its early explorations, otherwise there is the danger of it hanging itself.

If the cage is to house cats that are not clean, that is, which do not use the litter tray regularly, neither sand nor grass should be used, but the entire floor should be concrete. In this case, clumps of grass, or pots or trays of grass should be placed at regular intervals. With a concrete floor, boards of adequate size should also be supplied for the cats to lie on. If the cats lie with their backs against the wall, then boards should be placed against the wall up to a height of approximately 150 mm (6 in), to protect the cats' kidneys.

The outdoor pen should be sunny, but must also provide adequate shade during the daytime. Perpetual, glaring sunlight is neither good for adult cats nor for kittens. A small tree in front of the pen is an ample source of gently shifting shade. The inside chambers must be large enough for the owner to be able to clean them, and constructed of a material that can be readily disinfected. They should at all times be well aired, but free of draughts, and preferably admit daylight. To house four cats the minimum area of the external enclosure should be approximately 10 sq m (12 sq yd) and about 1.80 m (6 ft) high. Winter temperatures will, of course, depend on the variety of animal, and what it is accustomed to. As a rough guide, it is recommended that for long-haired cats the indoor temperature should not be below 14°C (57°F) and not rise above 23°C (73°F), while for shorthairs the indoor temperature should be no lower than 18°C (64°F) and not above 25°C (77°F).

Without a cage, a cat can hardly be kept within the limits of its own garden. At the first onset of heat, if not before, all inhibitions are cast aside, and the cat will roam the entire neighbourhood. A fence 1.80 m (6 ft) high, with an upper edge sloping inwards at an angle of 45°, and even an electrified grazing wire fence will deter most cats only for a certain time. Sooner or later they will find some way of breaking out. Various cat owners

16

1   Mongrel or pedigree, all cats are
great individualists. Choosing one will
depend partly on looks and partly on
individual character.

2   Cleopatra of Ayudhya is the elegant name of this pedigree Silver tabby shorthair.

3   An orange-eyed White longhair (White persian). The black hairs on its forehead make it less than perfect. Long coats such as this require a great deal of attention.

4   Ears, eyes and even nose, are
concentrated on identifying a movement
in the grass. Given the chance, the
majority of domestic cats are keen
mousers. It was probably their rodent-
catching skills that led to their adoption
as domestic animals.

5/6   Cats love warmth, whether it is a
patch of sunshine, a warm boiler top or
the patch beneath a reading lamp, you
can be sure they will seek it out.
Perhaps it is evidence of an origin in a
warm climate that it seems so important
to them.

7   Fresh air and sunshine help to keep
cats happy and healthy and they will
enjoy being able to go outdoors.

12   A separate kitchen unit equipped with refrigerator, cooking hob and washbowl makes food preparation convenient and hygienic in a sophisticated professional cattery.

13   If circumstances permit a domestic pet should be allowed as free an existence as possible but in a breeding cattery the residents cannot be allowed to roam. These outdoor pens with branches and multi-platformed posts give plenty of space for exercise and fresh air when the cats emerge from their compartments in the background.

4 *Ears, eyes and even nose, are concentrated on identifying a movement in the grass. Given the chance, the majority of domestic cats are keen mousers. It was probably their rodent-catching skills that led to their adoption as domestic animals.*

5/6 *Cats love warmth, whether it is a patch of sunshine, a warm boiler top or the patch beneath a reading lamp, you can be sure they will seek it out. Perhaps it is evidence of an origin in a warm climate that it seems so important to them.*

7 *Fresh air and sunshine help to keep cats happy and healthy and they will enjoy being able to go outdoors.*

8/9/10 *Kittens are continually poised between apprehension of the unknown and insatiable curiosity. They carefully investigate everything as they explore a new environment.*

11 Even in the middle of a quiet grooming session a cat will break off to concentrate on the identification of an intriguing or unsettling noise.

12 A separate kitchen unit equipped with refrigerator, cooking hob and washbowl makes food preparation convenient and hygienic in a sophisticated professional cattery.

13 If circumstances permit a domestic pet should be allowed as free an existence as possible but in a breeding cattery the residents cannot be allowed to roam. These outdoor pens with branches and multi-platformed posts give plenty of space for exercise and fresh air when the cats emerge from their compartments in the background.

have, however, reported positive results with electrified fences. The cats very soon learn that if they try to climb over the fence, they will suffer a slight but nevertheless painful shock, and from then on they will keep away from the fence.

Even if we provide our cat with sufficient exercise, either in a cage or at liberty, we should never forget that it is at least as important to devote time to it. An isolated animal, no matter how much freedom it has to move, will soon begin to pine.

An hygienic and functional interior layout for a cat house that can be easily cleaned and gives the cats an interesting environment where they will be happy and healthy.

A piece of carpet wrapped around a post provides a scratching place, as the carpet becomes worn it can easily be replaced.

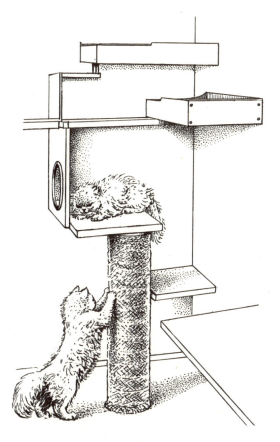

Ink and brush drawing by Joseph Hegenbarth

Aesop's Cat

Aesop's cat once was playing
With a little mouse.

'Run, little mouse!', said she and fondly
A claw at it; up and down   poked
She let it run, caught it again,
Cheerful and friendly was her mien.

'Ah, dear cat,' spoke the mouse,
'Well I know these flatteries
And these jokes. Poor little mouse,
They spell death for me.'

'What?' said the cat, 'You dare to mock!'
And bit it dead!

The short-haired domestic cat

The origin of the domestic cat

Specialists are not agreed either on the exact links between the members of the cat family or on the origin of the domestic cat, as we know it. What is certain, is that the relationships are close and that the domestic cat is descended from one of the wild cat species; exactly which one is still disputed. Wherever in the world smaller wild cats exist, crossings between them and the local ordinary domestic cats presumably occur. This applies to the native European wild cat. Prowling queen cats in season successfully mating with wild toms are a frequent occurrence. However, to conclude from this that all these sub-species are in some form the ancestors of the domestic cat would be a mistake. It is probable that several thousand years ago there was one central area where domestication began, but that there are also several different sub-species of the wild cat which may be regarded as the ancestral forms. Some authorities present the primary markings of the coats of embryo European domestic cats, which show stripes and not spots, as evidence for the theory that our European domestic cat is descended from the African wild cat. The domestic cat's marked preference for keeping itself warm and dry could support this theory.

The first stages in the domestication of the cat can be sought some 4,000–4,500 years ago in Ancient Egypt along the upper Nile. Until recently the sole original form was thought to be the local Kaffir cat, a light-coloured species, *Felis lybica*, from the north African desert wastes. Since early times this Kaffir cat has displayed a stronger association with man than any other sub-species of wild cat, including our European wild cat. The Kaffir cat is undoubtedly an ancestor of our domestic cat, but in all probability not the only one. Thus, a further possible ancestor is another wild cat, the creamy-grey African wild cat, *Felis ocreata*, from the highlands of Ethiopia.

It has been claimed that cats were kept in the Near East considerably earlier than in Egypt. The oldest known representations of cats from Anatolia, date from 6000 BC. Then statuettes were found at Hacilar, depicting women playing with cats, which suggested that cats have now been associated with man for more than 8,000 years.

Cats were found in excavations of sites in Jericho (Jordan) dating from the late sixth millennium or early fifth millennium BC. By the beginning of the third millennium BC, cats seem already to have been much more widespread. These regions were inhabited by further sub-species of wild cat, which may well have also been the original form in that area. It is very likely, however, that in all these early instances the cats must be regarded simply as tamed wild animals. For there is a distinct difference between mere taming, an accidental habituation to man, of which any animal is capable, and a continuing domestication process lasting over generations.

Finds of artifacts and paintings from the Badari culture in the Egyptian New Stone Age, dating from *c* 4000 BC, show that Kaffir cats were kept at that time. With the New Kingdom in Egypt, finds and representations become increasingly frequent, which suggests that cats were being introduced into the home, a genuine domestication. Egyptian tomb decorations depict the cat assisting at the hunt, as a pet, as a companion to man and as a divine symbol. Given the cat's territorial orientation, an important precondition of its domestication was, therefore, that the people seeking to achieve this should be settled in one place, which of course they were during Egypt's period of high culture. No doubt the cat was also tamed by nomadic tribes in many other parts of Africa, but this never amounted to true domestication.

It is, therefore, evident that between the time when cats are first known to have been kept and the point at which they became domesticated an intervening period of some thousands of years elapsed, far longer, that is, than for any other domestic animal. This may be attributed to the known fact that the cat is not sociable, but lives an aloof, independent life. The presence of the domestic cat in Crete some 4,000 years ago (*c* 2000 BC) has been established, as has its presence in China some 2,500 years ago, where it was introduced by way of India.

The house cat appears in ancient Chinese literature of about 800 BC. Like the tiger, which destroys the wild boar in the open country, the cat is revered as sacred for its extermination of destructive mice. Moreover, at this time the cat is a symbol for longevity. Throughout successive dynasties until approximately 200 BC, the strangest rites accompanied the worship of the cat and the tiger.

In Ancient Greece the cat does not seem to have been very common but in Roman times it became more widely known and spread throughout the empire. Domestic cats were probably introduced into England by Roman colonists.

If we try to discover the reasons why the wild cat should have become a domestic animal, we meet with widely differing causes according to the historical period and the individual country.

The domestic cat in history and legend

When, some 4,000 years ago, the Middle Kingdom Egyptians moved southwards up the Nile to attack the fabled land of Kush (Nubia), to seize the gold that was to make Egypt rich, they also encountered there the Nubian Kaffir cat. Whereas the Nubians called it 'Gadiska', the Egyptians simply named it after its voice, 'Mu'.

It seems that the Kaffir cat was predestined to become a culture-follower, and searched man out of its own accord. We know, furthermore, that the settled Egyptian farmers were greatly afflicted by the severe damage done by mice and rats to their hard-won stores of grain. They were always dependent on whether the Nile would flood and briefly make the land fertile, or whether the mass of water from Central Africa would fail to reach them, resulting in aridity and drought. Thus, in order to survive, it was essential

28

A domestic cat with a coat patterned like that of a wild cat

for the Egyptians to store ample supplies in their granaries. Naturally these stores of grain attracted hordes of rodents. It was not long before the Egyptians discovered that these pests were the cats' favourite prey. This may have been what caused the cat to become an object of Egyptian cult worship as the 'protector' of their grain supplies.

The animal symbol associated with Sekhmet, the Egyptian goddess of war, was the lion, and from each of the newly conquered territories Egypt's armies would send back a likeness of the lion to their homeland. These were placed in temples and throughout the land as a representation of the goddess, an object of worship and a source of her protection. In the Temple of the Sun at Heliopolis the great god Ra was worshipped in the form of a cat. There, too, Sekhmet, the terrible Big Cat, was worshipped alongside Bast, the kindly little cat. Bast, at first also lion-headed, was later visualised as a cat-headed woman.

Cats soon came to be so highly valued that, if fire broke out in a house, the cat would be the first to be rescued. When a cat died, the owners would cut off their hair or shave off their eyebrows as a symbol of mourning. The main shrine of Bast was in Bubastis, the city of the goddess on the lower Nile, and here the cat was given particular honour and reverence, as a source of human good fortune and divine blessing. As the symbol of Bast, the cat goddess, it was worshipped as the guardian of the home, and protector of women and children. In later times, her divinity was extended to make her goddess of elegance, grace, coquetry, sensual love and pleasure. Even when the Pharaohs burst upon Egypt in *c* 1000 BC, and 500 years later when the Persians invaded under King Cambyses, the cat goddess was spared and her cats continued to be worshipped as before.

History relates how, in the course of this Persian attack on Egypt, reverence for cats proved fatal for the brave Egyptians defending the vital fortress of Pelusion. After countless vain attempts to take the fortress by storm, the Persians hit on the cunning idea of seizing all the living cats they could find and strapping them to their shields. The Egyptians naturally did not dare to risk killing the creatures, and in desperation threw down their arms.

Herodotus, the historian, describes the ceremonies held in Bubastis in honour of the cat goddess in about 440 BC. Hundreds of thousands of pilgrims came from all over Egypt, bringing with them the mummies of any cats that had died in the past year. Encased in coffins of precious wood or precious metal, they were taken to the vast cats' cemetery at the feet of the goddess, for this was the only place where they could be buried.

After the end of the sixth century AD, the cat was profoundly revered and loved by the Prophet Mohammed. It is said that Mohammed cut off the sleeve of his garment, rather than disturb a cat which had fallen asleep on it. Mohammed is supposed to have singled out his closest followers with the honorary title 'Father of Cats'. However, in his frenzy to convert all around him, the same Mohammed was quite merciless towards his enemies, causing many heads to roll. Today the cat is still regarded as sacred by Hindus and Muslims, and is probably the only animal revered by members of both religions.

Domestic cats were comparatively rare in Greece and Rome until approximately the beginning of the Christian era. The Greeks and Romans preferred the weasel for dealing with rodents. Admittedly, furriers everywhere included cats' fur in their wares as we learn from the writers of Greek comedies. The Greek goddess Artemis later succeeded to the place of Bast, as protectress of women and goddess of childbirth. The celebrated Artemis grotto near Beni-Hassan-el-Amar contains numerous cat burials and images of Bast.

By way of Greece and Rome, where it was the symbol of freedom, the cat reached Central Europe, and here it was considered as a gift of great rarity. At that time, if ever a court surrendered to an enemy, then the cat would be listed—by name—along with the other entries in the inventory. However, it was its prodigious fertility, which from a breeding point of view was of course a great advantage, that very soon led to a decline in its value. Wherever corn was planted and stored after harvesting, and wherever a town was in danger of siege and starvation, the cat was highly prized as a rodent exterminator. In the Middle Ages a cat-worshipping Freyja cult still persisted. In 1484 Pope Innocent VIII issued a papal bull to put a stop to this. Cats fell into disfavour. During the Inquisition they even came to symbolise the devil and frequently met their end burned with witches and heretics at the stake. Hatred of cats became a cult. During the 150 years of the Inquisition, 30,000 witches and magicians and thousands of cats died in the flames. Even today popular superstition links the cat with all kinds of properties of fortune telling, sorcery and malevolence. Just think how many British people there are who believe a black cat will bring them luck, while in other countries people worry if a black cat crosses their path from the wrong side, and watch out for rain if they see the cat eating grass and other such nonsense!

It was quite another reason that prompted the Archbishop of Cologne to issue a decree in 1747 against the poor cats in the villages of his domain. Their occasional depredations among small game on his estates disturbed him. The instructions of this Prince of the Church read as follows:

We, Clemens August, by God's grace Archbishop of Cologne, . . . do hereby announce and make known: Since it has been brought to Our notice and daily observation has informed Us, that the constant roaming of cats in field and forest has resulted in the snatching and consuming of young hares and partridges, to the detriment of the hunt, We are compelled to prevent any further such damage by commanding all subjects in Our archbishopric, regardless of rank, to cut off the ears of all cats in their possession, right back to the head, thereby hindering the cats from roaming and poaching in field and forest in all weathers. Upon the due issue of this command, every man, regardless of rank, is therefore obliged to act in accordance with it. Any cat owner, who, in the course of monthly controls, is found to have contravened this command, will pay for each instance of contravention a fine of one quarter Gold Gulden fine, to be remitted immediately ... Issued in Bonn, on the 12th May, 1747.

But despite all the persecution of the Middle Ages, the cat survived in Europe. Renaissance poets and philosophers restored the cat to favour. Today, in Rome, for example, there are some 140,000 stray cats living among the historic walls and ruins. They are one of the somewhat dubious tourist attractions. Old ladies, themselves often short of food, look after these poor creatures.

Domestic cats were introduced to North and South America by European colonists. Without the domestic cat, the settlement of North America would hardly have been thinkable. Only the cats kept the grain stores safe from attack by rodents. Each mission station raised its own cats. The waggon trains heading for new settlements always carried several baskets full of cats. Even the North American Indians took over the cats from the white settlers and came to value them. Cats were a valuable commodity throughout the West. Here and there cats even checked the spread of rat-borne typhoid and the plague, by consuming the carriers. The first cat to arrive in Paraguay from Europe fetched one pound weight in pure gold. Herrera, the Conquistador, weighed each cat that was brought to Peru in gold. But the superstition and belief in witches, prevalent in the Old World at that time, followed the conquerors to the New World, so that there, too, the cat sometimes met with hatred and persecution.

Origin and development of cat breeding

The temple cats were sacred, revered and pampered and bred copiously. Mutations occurred from time to time, especially in terms of colouring, and these in turn became the objects of further religious veneration. There are many parallel examples in the animal kingdom, for example, the sacred 'white' elephants of India. Thus red, white and tortoiseshell cats appeared as mutations of the wild cat, but if the animals had been allowed to roam freely, they would soon have died out again, as a result of natural selection. Once man began breeding cats, a greater variety of shapes, colourings, patternings and length of hair appeared than are present in the wild cats from which they originated. Admittedly, until recently, selective breeding of cats consisted solely in permitting only one or possibly a few kittens of a litter to live, usually the strongest or, in subjective terms, the 'finest' or 'prettiest'.

As a rule ordinary house cats of either sex do not normally carry genes which are homozygous for a particular coat colour and patterning, but are heterozygous, which means they carry the characteristics of both father and mother as well as a mixture of characteristics. Consequently the appearance of each kitten will differ from that of its siblings, and also from that of its mother and its father. Certain colours and patternings predominate over others, i.e. they are either dominant or recessive. Which factors pro-

31

duce the dominant ones and which the recessive can only be discovered in the course of breeding. In the house cat the three-colour marking is usually sex-linked to the female. It seldom appears in domestic toms.

14 A Japanese woodcut of a tri-colour bobtailed cat trying to catch a butterfly

Unfortunately our understanding of the specific genetics of the domestic cat is still very limited. This is because the earliest records of the planned breeding of pedigree cats, first in Britain and subsequently in Europe, go back no further than the middle of the last century. The world's first cat show was held in the Crystal Palace, London, in 1871 but it was not until 1887 that the first major cat club was founded: the National Cat Club, which introduced a register and stud book for the British. It was followed more than a decade later by the creation of a rival club but a later amalgamation created the Governing Council of the Cat Fancy which controls the registration of cats, the recognition of breeds and the organisation of shows throughout Britain. Similar organisations have followed around the world.

Black (or melanism) was certainly one of the first gene mutations to develop from the original wild tabby. It is recessive only to the tabby, and dominant over almost all lighter shades. Blue is virtually black with a gene for dilution. It pales in certain crossings. Renewed crossings with black can restore this colour.

White occurs either simply as hair without pigmentation, or, more rarely, as skin without pigmentation. This is known as albinism, and the former type is far more likely to occur partially, that is, restricted to limited patches on the body, rather than all over. This albinism begins with patches on the throat, breast or stomach, extending to the shoulders and the flanks, and finally spreading all over. It is mostly dominant in breeding. Both partial as well as total albinism of the skin differs from albinism in the hair, even if both carriers are pure white. They normally still have the same colour eyes as cats of other colours. An unmistakable indication of albinism in all-white animals is the characteristic red albino eye. The thin, colourless iris allows the blood vessels of the *fundus oculi* to show through, thus making the eye appear red. However, albino cats, whose albinism can also be coupled with deafness, have an iris so thick that when a light is shone on to it in darkness, it will reflect red, but not in normal lighting conditions. Thus the pigmentless iris of the albino cat appears blue.

It is worth pointing out here that the reason why normal young kittens all appear to have blue eyes when they first open their eyes, is that pigmentation of the iris does not develop fully until a little later.

Albinism is inherited only where both partners are albino, and will appear in all kittens out of one litter. Albinism is recessive to all other colours. It can happen that crossing two tabby parents without any sign of white on them may produce one or more albino kittens in an otherwise normally coloured litter, because the parents carry unsuspected albino genes.

Cats with a blaze of white on the face and on the nose will consistently pass this on, regardless of the colour. Tabby patterned coats dominate over black, and may be mackerel striped or standard (blotched) tabby pattern. Mackerel or tiger stripes are clear, distinct stripes contrasting with the main colour, and encircling the body from the spine to the stomach. Breast and stomach are also marked with rings. The standard blotched

32

15 Although the short-haired domestic tabby has similar markings to the European wild cat and matings between the two have taken place it is not thought to be its primary ancestor.

16 The African wild cat is usually considered the most likely species to have developed into the domestic cat.

17 A bronze figure of a cat from ancient Egypt, where cats were treated with great respect and revered as the animal of the goddess Bast.

Overleaf:
18/19 All kittens are born with blue eyes, as they grow older the may change colour. The colour of the fur will also frequently get darker as the cat gets older.

20/21/22   *The permutations of colour and pattern in cats' coats are infinitely varied.*

23/24 *Enquiringly alert or calmly and critically surveying the scene, there is not much that eludes a cat's attention.*

25 Cautiously, this cat checks what is going on before entering a room.

26/27 Eyes and ears are constantly registering the slightest noise or movement. In the natural state a cat relies upon these senses most in detecting prey and for warning of any danger.

28/29 Cats are extremely agile even when balancing on their hindfeet.

30/31 When climbing a wall cats often seem capable of taking a second leap from a vertical position or pulling themselves up when there is no sign of anywhere to grip.

32 Their sure and uncanny sense of balance is aided by the conformation of their inner ear.

Overleaf:

33/34 Except for females in season and for screaming at an antagonist the cat makes little use of its miaow in feline communication but uses it to converse with humans.

35 Cats often establish a regular favourite spot to take a nap, to wash or to keep a look-out on the world's goings-on.

36 This playful roll on to its back actually puts a cat into a strong defensive position for it allows it to strike out with its powerful back legs.

37 *A cat may sit quietly for hours just watching the world from its observation place.*

38 *This cat's nictitating membrane, the 'third eyelid' which protects its eyes from excessively bright light and physical damage, is partly raised, which is often a sign of sickness, especially bad worm infestation. However it is always visible in some cats and the condition can be produced by such otherwise harmless causes as eating a large number of grasshoppers.*

tabby pattern, with whorls rather than stripes on the sides of the body, derives from a mutation of the tiger-striped markings of the ancestral coloured domestic cat.

Pedigree cats are only recognised in certain colours and patterns which are laid down by the registration bodies. The details sometimes differ from country to country and between associations. Some of the names and colours need explaining.

Tabby has already been described. Tabbies may be brown, silver or red, and in some cases blue or cream. Tortoiseshell markings consist of clearly defined patches of black, cream and red. There should be no tiger stripes and no white—tortoiseshell with white patching forms a separate breed.

'Red' is usually an orangey colour; 'cream', a lighter form of red, implies a shade in between the colour of dairy cream and cognac. 'Silver' is produced when a cat is more black than white, 'blue' is a greyish colour, which is a weaker form of black. An animal is termed a 'chinchilla' if it has a white coat in which the very ends of the hairs have dark tips. A 'Smoke' is a cat, whose under-colour is light silver, with the tips shading to reddish-black. Self-coloured cats—cats of an all-over colour—should not show any tabby markings. 'Agouti' or 'Ticking' is a touch or tip of one colour on the end of a hair of another colour, such as on Abyssinians.

A cat is considered homozygous if it carries the same genes as mother, father, grandparents and great-grandparents. From the breeder's point of view, these are the genes that affect the breed characteristics required by the current standard, such as type, colour and condition of coat. The external appearance of a cat—its phenotype—need not accord with its genetic picture—its genotype, as we have already seen when discussing albinism.

The commonest method of planned breeding of pedigree cats is the mating of animals with matching genes. This includes inbreeding, in which related animals of first and second degree are mated, that is mating of parent with offspring, grandparent with grandchild and brother with sister. Mating of related animals up to sixth degree is also considered to be inbreeding. In line breeding, the queen is paired with a first-class stud cat, and the offspring are then again paired with each other, so that they all go back along the same line. This type of selective breeding can easily produce degenerative traits, that is to say bad or defective features can be inherited as well as good ones, along with hereditary diseases. In such cases a very remotely related partner must be found from the same breed.

Another form of breeding is crossbreeding, namely the pairing of two animals of different breeds. The resulting litter will inherit the different characteristics of their parents in varying proportions. Displacement crossings seek to breed out undesirable characteristics over several generations, and refinement crossings attempt to introduce certain new features. Combined crossing of two or more breeds over an extended period will eventually produce new breeds with combined features.

Systematic breeding of the domestic cat according to skills and aptitudes—as with the dog—has never been achieved. Some breeders have attempted to maintain a particularly pleasant temperament in a strain but, for the most part, pedigree cats have been bred solely for their looks.

Short-haired cats are known in two basic types: the 'cobby' short-legged, solidly built cat, which for centuries was the prevalent form among the domestic cats of Europe, and the thin, long-legged and lissom 'oriental' type. Within those two broad groups there are a number of breeds with minor variations from the overall type, sometimes deliberately created by breeders, sometimes accidental. A great number of the non-pedigree domestic cats of Europe show the influence of the 'oriental' conformation and in America the basic 'cobby' type has been modified so that the American shorthair differs in several ways from that recognised in Britain and continental Europe.

The American shorthair, or Domestic shorthair as it is also known in the United States, has longer legs than the European cat, a longer nose and a more square muzzle—and it is recognised by the registration bodies in a wider range of colours than the Europeans have. In current pedigree breeding the general standard for all forms of European and British shorthairs favours the very active, muscular types. The Governing Council of the Cat Fancy (GCCF) in Britain, the Fédération International Féline Européenne (FIFE), an umbrella organisation for the majority of the continental bodies, a number of independent associations in North America and affiliated groups all over the world decide on what the acceptable standards for each particular breed will be. The different bodies do not always come to the same decisions, either about standards or as to whether a type shall be recognised as a separate breed at all. Some of the differences are pointed out in the catalogue at the end of this book. The situation is not a static one. New breeds are developed and recognised and changes in taste lead to revision of existing standards.

The Bi-coloured shorthair is a case in point. The Black-and-white, or Magpie cat as it used once to be known, had to have a very strictly controlled pattern and a later requirement, while accepting the colours black and white, blue and white, orange and white and cream and white, laid down that the patches of colour should be arranged like those of the Dutch rabbit. The face was to have a white blaze dividing it exactly and continuing over the head to the back of the skull. The ears and mask were to be coloured and the colour had to begin again behind the shoulders and continue down the back to include the tail and hindlegs. Hindfeet, forelegs and feet, neck, chin and lips had all to be white. This standard proved so difficult to meet that it was changed in Britain in 1971, with FIFE following suit, to allow a much more free disposition of the patching.

The orange-eyed British Blue is a heavy, thickset shorthair that probably most frequently comes closest to the ideal standard for the short-haired type. An almost identical cat, the Chartreux, so called because it was said to have been introduced from Africa by Carthusian monks, had long been known on the Continent and both are now considered to be the same breed. This robust, undemanding cat with greyish-blue to dark blue fur, has a temperament somewhere between the tranquil Persian and the lively Siamese. A further advantage is its very soft voice and it is claimed that it has an extremely short period on heat—sometimes as little as four days.

Another blue breed is the Russian Blue, first known in Britain as the Archangel Blue, supposedly because it had been brought to Britain in about 1860 by sailors coming from that Arctic port. Indeed, there are reports of a blue Archangel, which may have been very similar, brought back by sailors in the Russian trade as long ago as the reign of Elizabeth I. Cats of this breed are, like the British Blue, very tranquil, gentle and quiet in voice. Even when on heat they are much less noisy than other breeds. By contrast with the British Blue's broad, round head and cobby, massive body, the Russian Blue has a long, flat head and an elegant, raised, elongated and graceful body. The eyes are green, whereas the British Blue has yellow- or orange-coloured eyes.

The names of pedigree breeds do not necessarily have any connection with their geographical origin, or even with their descent. The Abyssinian, for instance, although claimed by some to be a direct descendant of the cats of Ancient Egypt, is largely the result of careful crossbreeding in Britain. Their agouti (ticked hair) markings are very similar to those of some North African wild cats, and a cat taken home by a British military expedition to Abyssinia in 1868 probably played its part, but the characteristic barring of each hair with two or three bands of colour does occasionally occur in ordinary tabby litters. Abyssinians have a reputation for being very devoted to their owners and energetic mouse- and rat-catchers. They tend to have small litters and consequently are comparatively rare.

The Havana or Chestnut Brown Shorthair does not hail from Cuba either, but owes its name to its cigar-like, chestnut brown colour. Foreign-type cats with a brown coat had appeared earlier but the first of the modern Havanas was born in 1952, as a result of a crossbreeding between a Chocolate point Siamese and a solid-coloured cat, but to produce the colour both cats must have carried the gene for chocolate colour. It was given official recognition as a breed in 1958. The Havana is highly individual, yet sociable towards man and its own kind. It differs from the Chocolate point Siamese in its single, even colour, and its green eyes. The eye colour is the most difficult factor in breeding Chestnut Browns. As with Russian Blues, there is always the tendency towards yellow eye colour.

Without any doubt, the best known of all shorthair pedigree cats is the Siamese. It really does appear to have come from Thailand although it may not have originated there and its appearance has changed somewhat since it was introduced into Europe. The first pair of Siamese cats is said to have arrived in England in 1884. It was claimed that its development was closely linked with the Siamese court but the breed is no longer easy to find in Thailand. Whether the Siamese was originally the product of a crossing between a fawn-coloured cat and the Bengal cat commonly found in Thailand remains a matter of some dispute.

The Siamese are elegant, slender, medium-sized cats, which become very devoted to their owners. Years of careful breeding have successfully eliminated some hereditary defects, such as squinting, the 'kinked' tail, stripes in the coat, and the 'round head'. They are temperamental, agile and very lively and consequently not ideal for a small flat. The Seal point Siamese are probably best known of all, with mask and points—that is face, ears, paws and tail—seal brown. Their body colour is cream shading to warm fawn on the back. The mask is complete, and connected by tracing to the ears. Kittens are much paler, even white. The cats become progressively darker under cold conditions and as they grow older.

The Blue-pointed Siamese has blue-grey points with a glacial white body colour. For breeding purposes, it is best to use a stud tom with very little Seal point in his ancestry. Blue point Siamese are supposed to be more affectionate than the Seal point. Too much sunlight can produce a light ash colour in the coat. With show cats precautions should be taken to avoid this, particularly immediately prior to exhibiting.

The Chocolate point Siamese is ivory all over, except for the points which are chocolate. The points of the white Lilac point are frosty grey with a pinkish shimmer. The colour of the Tabby point Siamese may be that of any of the varieties with solid-colour points but the tabby points have clearly marked stripes. At one time these were known as Platinum Siamese in Germany, and as Lynx or Shadow Siamese in England. However Tabby point Siamese is the name that best expresses their genetic background. The striped points are dominant over all other points in Siamese cats. Red point Siamese were first given breed recognition in England in 1966. Their body colour is white, possibly shading to pale cream, with bright red points. Since this red colouring is probably linked with ghost stripe or band markings, breeding pure specimens is a problem.

Another cream-coloured cat is the Tortie point Siamese, which has tortoiseshell points, which are seal brown broken with cream and red and a Cream-pointed cat has also been given a provisional standard.

Further solid-colour variations have been developed from the Siamese and the Havana has been joined by lilac and white cats of foreign type but, like the Havana, these are not known as Siamese. Many North American bodies also exclude the Tabby point, Red point and Tortoiseshell point from the Siamese group and describe them as Colorpoint shorthairs (not to be confused with the British Colourpoint).

The Korat is another cat that definitely comes from Thailand; it gets its name from the Korat Plateau where it is found. It is an attractive silver-blue cat, slightly more low-lying than the Siamese and with a rounded tip to its tail. It has an appealing heart-shaped face and fur which an old poem describes as having roots like clouds and tips like silver. In its homeland it is known as the Si-Sawat and is thought to bring good luck.

The Burmese breed had its origin in a hybrid Siamese, and European standards still expect a cat of foreign type, but it should be a more compact cat with a rounder head which now looks quite different from the Siamese type. In the United States round feet and round eyes are also now expected. Nevertheless, morphologically, genetically and ethologically—that is, in behavioural terms—the Burmese still retain many similarities to the Siamese. They are chiefly known with coats of sable brown or blue but a number of other colours have been produced. For the amateur it is not always easy to distinguish the Brown Burmese from the Havana or the Blue Burmese from the Russian Blue. Burmese kittens are much paler than the adult cats and still show a marked contrast between body colour and the points. This contrast reduces to a minimum at about 15 months.

52

The Rum Tum Tugger

The Rum Tum Tugger is a Curious Cat:
If you offer him pheasant he would rather
    have grouse.
If you put him in a house he would much
    prefer a flat,
If you put him in a flat then he'd rather
    have a house.
If you set him on a mouse then he only
    wants a rat,
If you set him on a rat then he'd rather
    chase a mouse.
Yes the Rum Tum Tugger is a Curious Cat—
    And there isn't any call for me to shout it:
        For he will do
        As he do do
            And there's no doing anything about it!

The Rum Tum Tugger is a terrible bore:
When you let him in, then he wants to be out;
He's always on the wrong side of every door,
And as soon as he's at home, then he'd like
    to get about.
He likes to lie in the bureau drawer,
But he makes such a fuss if he can't get out.
Yes the Rum Tum Tugger is a Curious Cat—
    And it isn't any use for you to doubt it:
        For he will do
        As he do do
            And there's no doing anything about it!

The Rum Tum Tugger is a curious beast:
His disobliging ways are a matter of habit.
If you offer him fish then he always wants
    a feast;
When there isn't any fish then he won't
    eat rabbit.
If you offer him cream then he sniffs and
    sneers,
For he only likes what he finds for himself;
So you'll catch him in it right up to the ears,
If you put it away on the larder shelf.
The Rum Tum Tugger is artful and knowing,
The Rum Tum Tugger doesn't care for a cuddle;
But he'll leap on your lap in the middle
    of your sewing,
For there's nothing he enjoys like a horrible
    muddle.
Yes the Rum Tum Tugger is a Curious Cat—
    And there isn't any need for me to spout it:
        For he will do
        As he do do
            And there's no doing anything about it!

House training

Cleanliness

We have already observed several times that cats are extremely clean by nature. This emerges plainly from their intensive grooming habits. The scrupulous cleanliness they maintain in their nest, or sleeping quarters, and particularly the way in which the mother keeps her kittens clean, reveals their instinctive fastidiousness. In the wild, the feral cat buries its excreta and urine, obliterating all trace of smell. From a very early age, kittens are normally already instinctively clean. In an artificial environment, that is, inside the house, the owner has to train the cats to deposit excreta and urine only where the owner wants them to. It is essential to begin this training from the moment when the kittens start taking food in addition to their mother's milk, for at this point the mother ceases to remove the kittens' droppings. This occurs at the very earliest at four to five weeks, but mostly not until the kittens are five to six weeks old. At all events, the kittens should be introduced to the virtues of cleanliness at a very early age. For the mother cat to carry her kittens to the litter tray is exceptional. Occasionally the kittens imitate the behaviour of the mother. If the mother does not 'train' her kittens, as soon as they are seen to take up the stance in which they relieve themselves, the owner should pick them up and place them in the litter tray.

The house cat will normally urinate twice or four times within a 24-hour period. The normal urine colour is yellow, and it may be slightly cloudy. Only the urine of adult uncastrated males has a strong and penetrating smell. Unless erect, the penis points backwards, so that the urine is directed in a backwards direction. Cats' excreta varies considerably in colour and firmness according to the food they have eaten. Urination and defecation are performed in a squatting position, the cat having previously dug a hole, and when it has finished, after sniffing, it will carefully cover over the hole with earth.

There is usually little problem in teaching a cat to use a litter tray indoors, for it will usually be the only place where it can go through these actions, and the cat is basically a very clean animal. If a kitten has already been trained to use a tray you may only have to show it where the tray is for it to know what is required.

First stage   If a kitten is not already using a litter tray the initial training should consist of taking the kitten several times a day, at regular intervals, and placing it on the tray. The position of the tray should be chosen carefully, so that it will not be necessary to change it. For a newly acquired cat, who is not yet familiar with its surroundings, it is best to select a quiet and concealed spot, otherwise the newcomer may attempt to perform its toilet in a dark place, offering cover, such as under a cupboard. If it already uses a tray an almost certain way to success is to ask the previous owner for a little of the contents of its litter tray. By placing this in the new tray, it will acquire the familiar individual odour of the cat, and there should hardly be any problem. A small kitten could be offered a choice of trays, each filled with different substances. Garden soil, sand, wood chips, peat, shredded paper, cellular pulp and bird sand have all been used but the proprietary makes based on types of clay are much more convenient, though expensive. They are highly absorbent and often help deodorize the tray. If the tray is lined with newspaper and the litter scattered on top it will make it go further. Disposable litter boxes are more often used for travelling or shows. However, the simpler and more 'modern' these matters become for us, the more unnatural, and complicated, and sometimes even unacceptable they become for the cat. Wooden or cardboard boxes are unsuitable as litter trays, since they absorb urine, and cannot be cleaned properly. Plastic trays of a convenient size are available from pet stores and are easily cleaned. The tray should not be too small, giving the cat enough room to move about a little, if it wants to, so that it does not find itself tipping the litter over the edge immediately it starts scratching it. Some cats will use sinks or even toilet bowls of their own accord, for their own toilet. Naturally, this simplifies matters, and some people even attempt to train the cat to do so. Of course, owners who are able to let their cat outside regularly may not always need a tray but if a cat is sick or has to be kept indoors it will be necessary to have one. **54**

Cleaning the litter tray   Cats can usually use their litter tray a number of times before the litter needs to be replaced and the tray cleaned. A few cats will, however, refuse to use a tray again, after only one use. In this case, the tray must be cleaned after each use or two or three trays could be placed near each other. For cleaning, use a long-handled brush, a cleaning agent, a solution of hot water and vinegar, or in obstinate cases a formalin solution. Three to five drops of eucalyptus oil added to the litter will suppress unpleasant odours for a while, and will not usually disturb the cat. Strong disinfectants should, however, be used only as a repellent to prevent the cat from using a certain place again. Ammonia, Lysol or even pepper will have the same effect.

Very occasionally cats do present a problem with house training. There are cases where a cat will be persistently unclean and despite all attempts at training will continue to do its 'business' in dark corners, on carpets or on covers, or other prohibited places. The only solution is to keep it out of doors in an enclosed pen or loose in the garden. Whether such an animal should be allowed to breed is a dubious question. Moreover, if it comes to selling or giving the cat away, the information that it is dirty must not be withheld.

Causes of dirtiness in a cat   There are a variety of reasons why a cat may be temporarily or even periodically dirty. However, it is a symptom that should be taken seriously, indicating that the cat is either physically or psychologically unwell. The most obvious physical cause would be an illness such as a bladder or liver disorder, stomach or intestinal upset, or an attack of endoparasites. The cat should be taken to the veterinary surgeon. Physical infirmity caused primarily by age could also be the cause. Punishment in these instances is pointless and would probably lead to the cat becoming permanently dirty. As soon as the cat regains its health it will also become clean again.

It is a little more difficult with psychological causes, which are not always clearly determinable. A cat that is normally clean, may become dirty just as a result of being in an unfamiliar environment, such as a clinic, or during a short stay in a cattery, or as a result of moving house and sometimes even after the contents of its owner's home have been rearranged. Ill treatment or neglect by the owner, such as leaving the cat alone for a long time in the house, putting the cat temporarily in someone else's care, the separation of cats accustomed to each other's company, the acquisition of a new, strange cat or even some other domestic animal by the household, ignoring the cat or even an addition to the family can trigger off this type of misconduct.

The effect of stress, such as the first vaccination, heat in the mother cat, a fight with a dog, an occurrence in the sexual area or the like can also produce temporary dirtiness. The cessation of the event producing such conflict will usually restore the cat to its previous clean habits. In unfortunate cases, however, the abnormal conduct may persist.

Incorrect training may often have a negative effect. To make a cat dirty is very quickly done, but to restore it to being clean can often be a long, laborious task. With young animals, in particular, it is essential to take great care to place them in the right place at the right moment. Praise and encouragement and gentle stroking have a positive effect. If toilet training proves difficult, then the animal should be kept for a few days in a wire cage which contains a cat tray. If the kitten makes a mess, then immediate punishment, such as a loud exclamation of disgust or even a light smack should be given. It should be picked up by the scruff, shown the spot where it has misbehaved, scolded, and then carried to the litter tray, where one should attempt to reinforce a positive impression by praise and stroking. The reaction must follow quickly on the act to be understood. There is little point in rebuking a kitten for something it has already forgotten doing and it is a great mistake to rub the kitten's nose in the mess. The animal has no way of understanding the connection. The cat's fear and nervousness will inevitably be increased, and it will then continually try to relieve its needs secretly in dark corners.

Partial cleanliness in a cat is a very curious, albeit a rare occurrence. The cat may, for example, leave its urine very neatly in the cat tray, but try and deposit its excreta somewhere else. Using several litter trays has been found helpful in such cases. If the cat shows a preference for the wash-basin, bath-tub or shower, then leave these filled with a little cold water for a while.

Sympathy, understanding, patience and experimentation are essential in order to train a house pet properly, or to make it clean again.

The widely known 'spraying' or marking has nothing to do with being dirty. Almost all uncastrated males will mark as a means of indicating territory and to attract females. The process is to a certain extent part of a mutual advertisement as to their physiological condition, their readiness to mate. The female in heat is likewise given to this kind of spraying and may occasionally leave a puddle.

Those who wish to keep cats in a manner appropriate to the animal's way of life, care for them properly and train them well, must be familiar with their natural behaviour and their needs. The well-being of our pets frequently does not coincide with the notions and preconceptions we have. Pet owners always seem tempted to humanise their animals, and to judge them in the light of their own feelings and emotions. The instinct-bound behaviour of animals, their drives and inhibitions can never be assessed or graded in terms of intellect, let alone virtue. To do so would be to do the animals a disservice.

The behaviour that a cat displays towards us is the same as that directed at members of its own species, that is to say, the cat simply treats us like another 'cat'. It displays its social grooming behaviour to us: its 'cat' greeting, by extending its head, its courting behaviour when it is in season, it rubs itself against our leg on encountering us, and much besides. The behaviour of the cat, like that of every other species, is only intended to be understood by its own kind. Calls, expressive behaviour and mimicry are understood and answered correspondingly only by its own kind. Animals of a different species mostly do not understand these signals and may even misinterpret them if the same or similar behaviour pattern exists in their own species, since it probably has a completely different meaning. This is why there are unfortunately such frequent misunderstandings between cats and dogs, which we will discuss more closely later.

The same is true of the person who is not really familiar with the behaviour of the cat, does not understand it and thus equates its behaviour with his own pattern of behaviour and emotional responses, humanising it and consequently totally misunderstanding it. This frequently gives rise to fundamental errors in his attitude to the cat, its care and training. In extreme cases, the dividing line between love of animals and cruelty to animals is a very narrow one.

However, if we really understand our pet cat and interpret its expressive behaviour correctly, we will quickly gain the trust and affection of the animal. Were I a keeper in a zoo, for example, whenever I passed the Siberian Tigers' enclosure on my daily round I would never fail to speak softly to each one of the tigers in turn, and greet them with the snuffling sound typical of their own greeting. The tigers would instantly respond in the same manner, and soon I would be accepted as a 'fellow-tiger', i.e. a trusted member of the species. However, if I were to greet the tiger loudly and produce a snarling sound, I would make the tiger aggressive and unapproachable.

Patience and consistency   The training of a cat, or any other animal for that matter, requires patience and calm. Just speaking quietly to it, and using steady gentle movements will help build up the desired trust. Incessant loud commands, or shouting at the cat and rushing about erratically, will soon reduce it to a fretful, nervous and aggressive creature, and can even make it thoroughly timid and withdrawn. Right from the start, get the kitten used to a particular order and routine. The kitten, itself, does not like finding its tray or its basket put in a different place each day. Being fed, played with and, where possible, let out, and also sleeping at regular times suit the natural rhythm of the animal's life, and adjustment to the times we choose will not take long.

A lot of time spent playing with the kitten will be enormously appreciated. Young kittens, in particular, will play tirelessly. By providing this outlet, we give the kitten the activity it may otherwise lack. Apart from aiding physical development, playing with the kitten can also include a certain amount of training. Accustoming it to a scratching post and to retracting its claws as it plays with people's hands, listening to commands and obeying calls can all be taught in play.

The extent to which the kind of humanisation mentioned earlier can be detrimental to a house pet is illustrated by the following example. We may think we are acting for the best by acquiring a second cat or even another pet as 'company' for an established cat that has lived in the house for years. However, this may drive the cat away from the house, or cause a behaviour problem. When acquiring a first pet, it is essential to decide on the range of pets we ultimately intend to keep. Young cats adapt quickly to each other, and can also be introduced to other pets without complication and a sibling pair acquired together will usually make good companions. To keep a number of cats in a city flat should certainly be an exception, and is only to be recommended to those with a large, enclosed garden, or where it is safe to let the cats run loose.

But even where they are permitted a free and unrestricted life, a large number of cats never really bonds into a group, a social unit. They get to know each other, and to respect each other according to a simple, uncomplicated hierarchy. As a rule, there is not even any fighting at the feeding bowl. However, a common unified activity never occurs.

House cats possess keen powers of observation, and there is no doubt that they learn from experience and apply this knowledge in their behaviour. They recognise instantly things that have caused them displeasure in the past, and immediately keep a safe distance. They have a well-developed sense of orientation, and will recognise places after weeks and even months. They will also recognise people they have trusted after prolonged separation. The time it takes them to forget varies considerably with the individual cat.

Cats and children   If there are children in the house, then there need never be any worry lest the cat should get bored. A child, like a cat, is insatiable when it comes to play. However, the difference between a toy and a live plaything should be explained to the child. It should be steered towards the kind of game that is appropriate for a cat, which leaves it sufficiently free. If the cat should decide it has had enough, it will simply disappear. For a child, a pet—no matter what kind—is a valuable enrichment of its environment. From the earliest age it is taught to love, respect and show consideration for the animal. If the child is given certain tasks to do under supervision, involving it in the care of the pet, this will develop self-confidence and a sense of responsibility. If the child is instructed beforehand about the life of the cat and its needs, it will then take the duties entrusted to it very seriously. We should, however, bear in mind that very often children's interest and accordingly their sense of responsibility flags very quickly. Care should be taken that the cat does not suffer as a result.

The runaway cat   If one day to the consternation of all concerned, your pet cat should be found to have escaped from the shelter of your four walls, the course of action to adopt is to go to work calmly and sensibly to retrieve the cat unharmed. Primarily the cat will have run away to escape from a place—be it a pen, an enclosure, a flat or a vet's clinic—not from people. Only if it finds itself being excitedly pursued by people, will it run away from them as well. If the cat has disappeared, there is little point in searching for it out of doors. It seldom runs straight outside, but finds the nearest hiding place, under the bed, in a cupboard, or behind the cooker. There it will wait quietly, but suspiciously, watching everything that takes place. If the cat was in fact, outside when it escaped, it is likewise not too difficult to catch it again, if you are familiar with its behaviour and act accordingly. When escaping, the cat will nearly always run in a straight line from its starting point to a nearby hiding place, without stopping. If up to now, you have been keeping your eyes on it, approach the cat slowly, but without looking at it. The cat will then stay seated where it is, and watch your actions with interest. Not until you are down on the same level as the animal, should you turn to it, and speak to it reassuringly. It will usually just crouch down, but may even come to you. To chase it wildly would be quite wrong.

Expressing mood   The means of expression available to the cat cover a wide range. The variations in their expressive behaviour are supplemented by mimicry and different noises. By these means any cat can very soon transmit its moods and feelings to someone familiar with it. If it rubs itself against one's legs, pushing its head against them, this is the cat's most affectionate form of greeting. Purring with satisfaction, it stretches out on one's lap. The slightest change of mood is indicated by the tip of the tail twitching, and the whole tail may wave to and fro with increasing vigour. In extreme agitation, the tail will slice through the air like a whip. Varying degrees of defensive stance are plainly indicated by flattened ears, growling and snarling and an arched back with the hairs standing up on end.

The familiar arched back of the cat is in fact the expression of wavering between moods of attack and defence. Menacing noises frequently reinforce these stances. It has often been observed that on the whole the cat can maintain friendlier relations with human beings than with animals of its own kind. Man is presumably not sufficiently 'cat-like' to provoke the defence reflexes in this highly individual creature.

Nothing varies in the individual cat so much as its temperament. Each transitional stage of every type exists, ranging from the most phlegmatic to the extremely sensitive and nervously agitated.

Obedience It is always more difficult to train a cat than a dog. The cat is certainly able to learn very quickly the meaning of several words, if these are always used in the same context, and preferably spoken in the same tone. The fact that it may often ignore being called is linked with its very distinct individuality. If one is not too insistent about it, however, the cat will, as it were quite casually, just happen to do our bidding. Mostly it has taken note of one's call, and somehow curiosity will make it come to one. A call at a regular time associated with food or games, will almost always be answered and other stimuli, too, such as banging the food bowl, imitated mewing, or a familiar rattling of a door will attract the cat. The kitten is highly discerning in its assessment of people. Even in the family, it will have 'favourites', while rejecting others completely. The main favourite is by no means automatically the one chiefly responsible for its care and providing its food. This curious selectivity emerges even more plainly with strangers, who visit the house. Some will be accepted instantly and greeted with affection, while others will prompt the cat to retreat timidly to the safety of open territory for no apparent reason. Mostly the cat will not have had any previous unfortunate experience with such persons. A variety of factors can be decisive, such as the appearance of the person, his demeanour, his voice or his smell. By trying to force the cat to greet this person, and acknowledge him, no one would benefit. Scratched hands and faces might be the least of the evils that would result.

Is the cat a bird-catcher? It often happens that the cat's hunting instinct is aroused as it sits by the window and watches the birds. In the long term this becomes a problem, if the family also keeps a feathered pet, such as a parakeet or a canary. And yet a kitten can usually very soon be trained to accept even this totally different kind of house companion. Time and patience spent at the very outset will save a lot of aggravation and argument. The cat rapidly understands that this particular bird is taboo as prey. All my cats, ordinary house cats and pedigree cats became so friendly with my birds that within a few days Pin-legs was permitted to ruffle their fur or hop about on their heads. Their instinct to stalk birds out of doors also diminished appreciably or even disappeared completely.

What is the truth about cats and bird-catching? Judging by its behaviour when stalking, the cat is not a bird-catcher, but a mouse-hunter. The stealthy approach, the lying in wait, preparation to spring, and the leaping on to the prey in themselves are so unsuitable for birds, that it is rare for a healthy bird to be caught. The way in which the bird

59

is continually on the move, hopping about all the time, constantly compels the cat to start its lurking ritual all over again. Consequently the bird is up and away before the cat is ready to spring. Even so, the bird that is occasionally caught by chance in disadvantageous circumstances, cannot compare with the millions of birds that are caught and killed every year by man in Continental Europe as they migrate southwards, or with the millions of birds that are inadvertently killed by pesticides and herbicides, or with the hundreds shot by airguns or the hundreds killed by speeding traffic on the roads. Crows, magpies, jays and many other nest-robbers destroy far more fledglings than ever cats do. The cats' commonest victims are sparrows and blackbirds, and these are species that breed quite prolifically. By placing water in an exposed position in the garden, where there is no cover, by leaving dead foliage under bushes, so that their rustling prevents the cat from creeping up undetected, and by attaching obstacles to prevent cats from climbing those trees where birds are nesting, it is possible to frustrate their opportunities for hunting from the start.

If a kitten is not permitted out of doors at all, care should be taken, for some cats will suddenly 'understand' how doors are opened. Without any prior training or indication, they may one day just jump up at the door handle, and use paw and head to widen the gap of the door as it opens, until they manage to slip through. After that no unbolted door will be safe from them.

The house cat should be strictly forbidden to nibble at food laid out on the table. This bad habit may be induced, should the kitten be given its food at the same time as the family. Even offering scraps from the plate is a mistake.

The bed is no place for either pedigree or house cat, the basic rules of hygiene should be enough to make this obvious. For all the cat's natural cleanliness, such indulgence still leads to an anthropomorphic attitude to the cat which is quite misapplied.

Sharpening claws Scratching with its claws on upholstered furniture, carpets, covers and curtains is not misbehaviour, but evidence of the poor training a cat has been given. Immediately the cat is offered a better alternative, such as a scratching post, and directed to it at the appropriate moment, it will very soon comprehend where it should perform this instinctive and very necessary grooming function. If a kitten is not taught where to scratch early on, it will be to the owner's extreme discomfort, for the fully-grown cat may attempt to do so on a trouser leg or even on stockings or tights. Even when it is seated on someone's lap and being fondled and stroked, so that it is purring loudly, suddenly the claws may shoot out unexpectedly producing scratches that draw blood. This has nothing to do with feline 'deviousness'. In a state of excitement, which may well be pleasure-induced, the claws are splayed out almost automatically. Even at the height of sexual arousal, as an expression of ecstasy the claws play a natural, not insignificant role in the behaviour of the mating cats. Jaroslav Stanek has put forward a further, altogether credible explanation for an alleged 'change of mood' in a cat. Stroking the cat produces an electrical charge in the fur. It may happen that the contact between the warm fur and the hands can result in a discharge, giving a shock to the highly sensitive nose or whiskers. The modern textiles that are in common use frequently produce a similar effect.

Dogs and cats It has already been stressed that members of a species employ a wide variety of bodily actions in their behaviour to communicate with each other. Animals of a different species frequently misinterpret these actions. Such misunderstandings often play a negative role between cat and dog. However, the assumption that there is an inborn enmity between cat and dog is quite without foundation. It depends entirely on the owner how a first encounter between the two species turns out. Even 'spoiled' animals can, with a little patience, be reconciled to become friends. The behaviour patterns of the two species are almost directly opposed. Whereas, for example, the dog begins a friendly greeting by wagging its tail furiously, if the cat lashes its tail, this indicates an extremely aggressive mood. In any encounter, the cat will remain watchfully at a distance, while the dog, particularly a young one, will hurl itself towards you in greeting, usually barking joyfully. The dog, originally a domestic hunting animal, persistently chases anything fleeing from it, while the cat will as a rule immediately take refuge in flight. Misunderstandings between the two are thus inevitable.

If the two are brought up together, both will become familiar with the other's characteristics and accept them up to a certain point. In this way many close friendships between dogs and cats may develop. However, it is also not too difficult to accustom adult animals to each other. The cat can be left in a high place such as the top of a cupboard, for example, to watch the dog playing and tearing about. The owner should not give the dog too much attention, to avoid arousing the 'jealousy' of the cat. After this the cat should be left to observe the play area alone and uninterrupted. Meanwhile, each animal should be given some object belonging to the other, to familiarise each with the other's scent. At this point an encounter between the two may be attempted, accompanied by much gentle encouragement and stroking. In so doing, it is best to restrain the dog who is always lively, and not to block off the cat's possible line of retreat. It is a good idea to bring the cat together with the dog when the latter is very tired or even asleep. Once the animals have made friends, they will always greet each other in a friendly manner, sleep together and even groom each other. Fighting over food virtually never occurs, even if only one bowl is used. However, at the slightest indication of any problem in this area, the cat should be fed in a separate spot.

61

One of the greatest errors an owner can possibly make is to set his dog at a cat or his cat at a dog. The existing friendship between one's own animals should not, however, be taken for granted with strange animals. Placing one's cat with a strange dog can produce a very different reaction indeed.

Pedigree and non-pedigree cats living in a modern household, especially in a large city, are frequently exposed to stressful situations, that is, to situations and dangers of various kinds that overtax the adaptive abilities of the cat. Some of these problems will be examined here. Its owner's annual holiday can be a particularly difficult time. In too many cases owners find their love for their pet fades at the thought of sacrificing a holiday to take care of them. Animal defence leagues and animal homes have a sad high season during the holiday period. The number of abandoned cats soars. Right from the outset, every animal owner should be clear in his mind as to how he is going to spend his holidays.

Environmental dangers

Some cats will adapt well to a temporary home and many make regular trips to weekend country and seaside homes with their owners but, if they are likely to be on the move, or going abroad so that quarantine regulations make them leave the cat behind, it must be cared for. If the owner has to travel for professional reasons it is most unlikely that the cat can be taken along. Ideally there may be friends prepared to come and stay to care for pets while their owner is away. Mostly, the cat will have to be entrusted to a friendly neighbour or left with people whom it knows well or in a boarding cattery.

It may be less disturbing for the cat to leave it in the house and to ask a friend to come in regularly to see that the animal is all right, to provide it with all that it needs, and to clean out the litter tray. A detailed list of all the things that need to be done for the care of the cat will help the cat-loving neighbour to remember everything.

A lot can also be done by carefully accustoming the kitten well ahead of time to having different people temporarily look after it. Never should a cat be let loose in the garden, or locked up in the cellar, for the duration of a holiday. In the USA and, since 1971, in the Federal Republic of Germany, a form of 'cat-sitting', akin to the ubiquitous baby-sitting has been in operation. A 'Sitters' head-office located in Dusseldorf already has over 50 helpers at its disposal who are prepared to go by the hour to the homes of cat owners who are away, in order to look after their pets.

Fortunately there are also good boarding catteries who will provide accommodation, food and general care while you are away. Veterinary surgeons may be able to recommend one or they may be listed in Yellow Pages. Inspect them to make sure that they maintain a high standard and, if you need to use them at popular holiday times, book well ahead, for places are often difficult to find in peak periods.

Cats will have to be healthy and immunised against Feline Infectious Enteritis before they will be accepted. Many cats benefit from a couple of weeks fresh air and change of outlook but elderly cats may find the jolt too great and suffer. Those devoted to their owners may mope for a day or two but soon recover their spirits with other cats about. If a cat gets used to a regular holiday home when it is still young there should be no problems.

advance of the proposed date of travel as to the regulations existing in the country of one's destination as requirements vary from country to country, in some cases requiring veterinary surgeon's and vaccination certificates (in some cases issued four weeks ahead of travelling), identification certificates and the like. Official veterinary surgeons, frontier authorities, cat breeders and, occasionally, travel agencies can provide the relevant information.

Although it should be avoided whenever possible, if it should ever be necessary for the cat to travel unaccompanied, either to a new owner, or for breeding or to a show, then a special label should be attached to the travelling basket, indicating that it contains a live animal. Do not forget to mark it clearly with the destination, the recipient's name, the sender's name, and with instructions to keep the consignment away from draughts, cold or intense sunlight. If arrangements have been made with the recipient, the docket should also be marked 'For Collection', and include the recipient's telephone number, in order to minimise the transportation time as much as possible. If a journey by air is involved, make detailed enquiries as to which airlines accept cats and under what conditions. Many have their own animal cabins, some insist on special travelling baskets, and there may be special instructions concerning delivery to the airport and collection.

Moving house When moving house, it is likewise advisable to attach collar, harness and lead to the cat. In all the upheaval of a move, it is best initially to lock the cat up safely in a quiet, unused room, until calm and order have been restored. Only then should you allow the cat to explore the new accommodation and all its facilities with you. The cat's old belongings should in any case have been brought, to facilitate acclimatisation to its new surroundings. Any necessary replacement of its things is best made gradually, and preferably not at the same time as its entire environment has been changed.

Car owners who keep cats should always observe certain precautions. Unfortunately, all too many cats are run over by their owners. Cats like to keep a look-out from under the safety of their owner's car, even sitting on the wheel beneath the mudguard. When

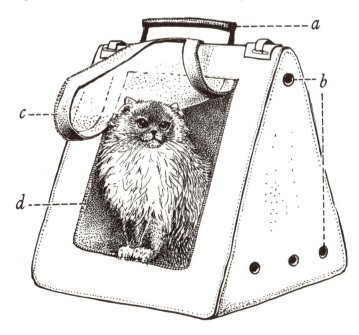

An original carrying bag, made in Germany, which has a transparent panel so that the cat can see out. Carried by a handle (a) and ventilated by holes (b) the opening is filled by a clear sheet of plastic (c) kept in place by a zip fastener around three edges (d).

A Siamese cat wearing a harness and lead

Cat and car   A further possibility would be to put the cat in the car and take it along on holiday with you, even if you are not staying in a holiday villa or cottage. There are some hotels and guest houses that will accommodate four-legged guests as well. Your travel agency will surely be able to supply you with the addresses of such hotels.

Cats usually take well to travelling by car. On short journeys they often enjoy watching the world go by, but on longer ones are best left to sleep in a closed container. Cats should never be left loose in the car, but should be placed in an enclosed basket, a well-ventilated box or at the very least secured by means of a collar or harness and a lead. Extremely practical, solid travelling baskets for both cats and dogs are available. Without such precautions, an accident can all too easily happen. Prompted by a playful impulse, or frightened by some sudden occurrence, the cat may suddenly leap onto the neck of the driver. Even when stopping briefly, and once the destination is reached, the lead should always be attached, since the cat could otherwise dash off in unfamiliar surroundings and get lost.

If the kitten is accustomed as early as possible to the wearing of a collar or a comfortable harness, and to being led on a lead, many problems will be avoided. This kind of training may be begun at between eight to nine weeks' of age. For car travel, it is necessary to have a bottle of fresh drinking water, a drinking bowl, the feeding bowl, dry or tinned food and, above all, the animal's usual litter tray.

The latter is particularly important, since many cats accustomed to a litter tray will often refuse then to relieve themselves out of doors. While staying in unfamiliar surroundings, it is an advantage to take the familiar grooming implements, the sleeping basket and similar accessories. It is an advisable precaution, not to give the cat anything to eat for four to six hours prior to travelling and to reduce the quantities of water for drinking. Its need to relieve itself will be reduced accordingly.

Before the journey   Clearly, overseas travel cannot be undertaken with a cat without complying with legal requirements concerning the import of animals and, if travelling to, or returning to a country such as Britain, with stringent quarantine regulations, it would be foolish to take a cat on holiday or short-term trips when it may have to spend much longer in quarantine than the duration of the trip. Enquiries should be made well in

41 A Tortoiseshell and white short-hair: centuries ago Americans and northern Europeans knew this type as a Spanish cat and the eighteenth-century naturalist Buffon thought that it owed its colouring to the Spanish climate.

42 A Tortoiseshell shorthair: This variety is almost always female.

43 A Blue Burmese: Burmese may have eyes of any shade of yellow but green eyes are not desirable. They are a serious fault in the Brown Burmese but a slight tinge is currently permitted in the Blue variety.

48   *A black and white Bi-coloured shorthair*

49   *A cobby conformation and squinting eyes would no longer be acceptable in a Siamese.*

50   *A good Siamese now has a wedge-shaped head. The whole body should give a long, slender and elegant impression.*

51 Black markings on a silver ground characterise the Silver tabby shorthair, which should have green eyes.

52 The Red tabby shorthair should have a deep orange-red coat with markings of an even darker red. Though often known as ginger or marmalade cats these terms do not accurately describe the colour required for cats of show standard.

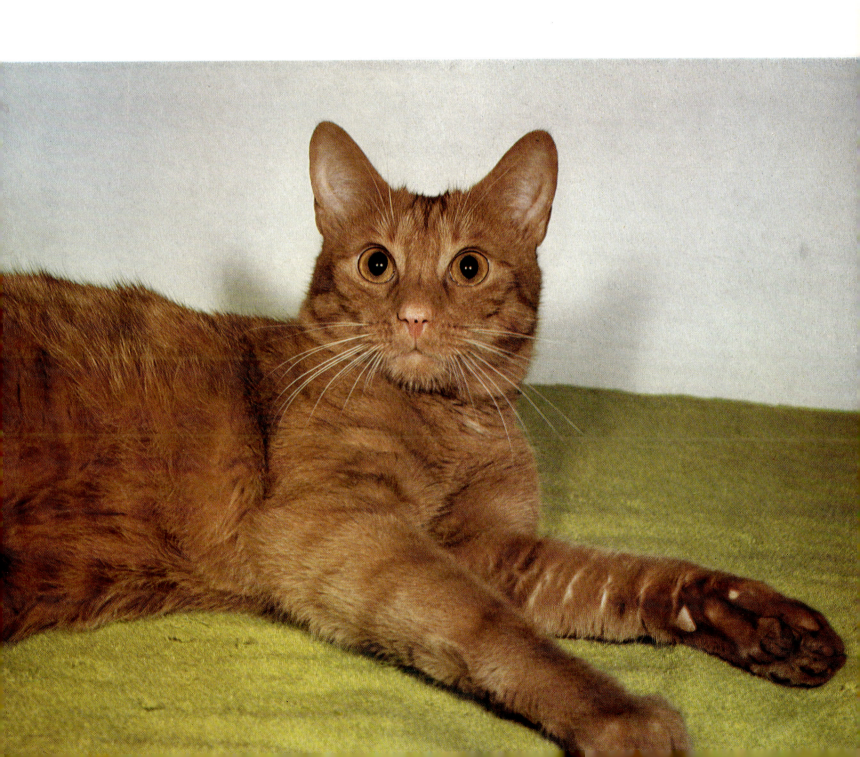

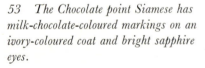

53 The Chocolate point Siamese has milk-chocolate-coloured markings on an ivory-coloured coat and bright sapphire eyes.

54 The Tabby point Siamese has clearly defined tabby markings on the mask and legs and along the tail. Its eyes are deep sapphire blue.

55 The Seal point Siamese with its deep brown points is probably the best known variety of Siamese and one of the most popular and most easily recognised of all pedigree cats. The kitten's markings will become stronger and more clearly defined as it gets older.

56/57 Although much sought after the Abyssinian cat is not so widely seen as the Siamese, partly because it usually bears much smaller litters. In a show cat the white area around the lips should be as restricted as possible. If it extends on to the neck it would count as a fault.

58 With wrinkled nose and bared teeth this cat is hissing a warning, but the erect ears show that the threat is still only a threat not an announcement of aggressive intent.

59   A mother cat will spend hours washing her kittens. The massage with her tongue also stimulates the function of the kitten's digestive system.

60   By the age of two weeks a kitten can already scratch behind its ears. This ten-week old kitten can perform the action easily.

61   Kittens at play use many of the physical signals of an adult confrontation. The flattened ears of the kitten on the right show that he means business, although not yet in a fully aggressive posture. His playmate shoots his paws out in defence and looks a little wary but is still reacting playfully. One rear leg is already poised to kick out if the attack should be carried further.

62/63 *Kittens can play for hours without becoming tired or bored. These Tabby longhairs are having fun with a table tennis ball on a piece of thread.*

64 Any dog owner who sets his animal after a cat is guilty of unpardonable behaviour. Lifelong hostility to dogs may be the result.

65 If they grow up with a pet bird as part of the home many kittens can be trained to accept it and live in harmony with it. This jackdaw's sharp claws and beak are a powerful defence against an inexperienced kitten which soon learned to show it appropriate respect!

66 Despite the hours they spend watching and stalking them, many cats prove poor bird-catchers, even though they may be efficient mousers.

67/68/69 *Cats and dogs that are reared together often become devoted companions. Correct training and care in the introduction of a new pet should ensure peaceful coexistence and may produce real friendships.*

the owner goes into the garage, the cat follows him and sits and waits in front of the garage. The cat can easily be run over by the reversing car. Likewise, never drive on to the premises or into the garage except at very slow speed, as the cat, who very quickly learns to distinguish the sound of its owner's car from that of other vehicles, may well be running to greet you. Particular care should be taken with young cats, ranging from six months to two years of age, since they are then still very playful, impulsive and enterprising, but, on the other hand, they are still careless and inexperienced. Sadly, cats are becoming ever more frequent victims of road traffic. It happens especially to those who are only seldom allowed out, and to those who are only out at night. In the dark, neither the cat nor the driver can accurately assess the speed at which the car is approaching.

Accidents in the home Accidents can just as easily happen inside the home. Cases continually crop up of cats being shut inside cupboards, drawers and even refrigerators. The animal is attracted either by the dark hiding place, or by the familiar source of food. It can disappear inside with lightning speed. Cats who have their own fixed 'lookout post' on a ledge by an open window or on a balcony, can fall off. All it takes is for some bird flying past to rouse the cat from dozing in the sun, and make it shoot up, and quick as lightning the damage is done. By erecting a thin, woven mesh of any virtually transparent material, the vantage point can be secured from all sides.

Open, tilting windows can be fatal, causing strangulation if the cat is jammed in the tilted window. Cats, and especially kittens, may try to play with electrical flexes, and should they bite into them, they can receive a fatal shock. If the owner, or a neighbour has a swimming pool in the garden, and the cat falls in, it could drown. Cats are, in fact, good swimmers, but they cannot climb a sheer side and may become exhausted before they can be rescued. A float should always be left on the surface of the pool, to provide a rescue raft, if necessary. If we constantly keep a watchful eye on our feline companion, and assess its abilities to adapt itself to the modern household and what goes on in it, we can do much to protect the kitten from mishaps, and ensure its safety.

Ink and brush drawing by Joseph Hegenbarth

James Kirkup   The Bird-Fancier

Up to his shoulders
In grasses coarse as silk,
The white cat with the yellow eyes
Sits with all four paws together,
Tall as a quart of milk.

He hardly moves his head
To touch with nice nose
What his wary whiskers tell him
Is here a weed
And here a rose.

On a dry stick he rubs his jaws,
And the thin
Corners of his smile
Silently mew when a leaf
Tickles his chin.

With a neat grimace
He nips a new
Blade of feathery grass,
Flicks from his ear
A grain of dew.

His sleepy eyes are wild with birds.
Every sparrow, thrush and wren
Widens their furred horizons
Till their flying song
Narrows them again.

Manx cats and other deviant forms

Fortunately cat breeding shows very little tendency towards abnormalities and mutations. The conscious or unconscious selection of kittens born in the same litter for breeding purposes plays an important role in this. Certainly the domestic cat might be expected to produce every possible symptom resulting from domestication and inbreeding, such as, for example, dwarfism and gigantism, legs of unequal length, absence of outer ears, pug-face, ring-tail and the like. In most instances, such attributes would indeed ruin the beauty of the cat. Fortunately few such abnormalities occur, but there are some breeds, developed from mutations, which are a matter of controversy. Although recognised by some registration bodies their perpetuation is frowned upon by other cat enthusiasts.

One obvious mutation has been a recognised breed since the early days of the Cat Fancy. That is the Manx, a tailless cat which takes its name from the Isle of Man in the Irish Sea. It has a hollow at the end of the backbone where the tail would normally begin. In addition the hindquarters are very high. This produces a rabbit-like, hopping gait and makes it more difficult for the cat to jump downwards. The absence of a tail is coupled with other deformities such as a shortened, oblique pelvis, deformed lumbar vertebrae, abnormalities in the muscles and nerves, and sometimes even a form of spina-bifida. It is also linked with a mortality factor: litters born of several generations of Manx-to-Manx matings, without out-crossing, frequently contain stillbirths or kittens that die soon after birth.

Not all Manx kittens totally lack the tail. Some have a shortened stump and others may even have a complete tail, but they would not be recognised as belonging to the true breed, although separated varieties have been recognised in Britain for stumpic and

87

tailed Manx. Stump-tailed cats also occur in other parts of the world, in Java and Sumatra they have been particularly reported. Perhaps they have some connection with the very short-tailed cat found in Japan, although the Japanese Bobtail, which appears in many famous Japanese paintings and prints, does not carry the lethal gene present in the Manx. The Bobtail actually has a tail four or five inches long but carries it curled in such a way that it looks much shorter.

Another deviant form which was reported from China long ago was a drop-eared cat. It was claimed that they were bred for eating. In 1961 a cat with pendant ears was produced in a farm cat's litter in Scotland and her kittens continued the abnormality; although at birth the ears appear pricked they begin to droop as the cat gets older. The GCCF has refused to recognise this as a breed in Britain but it has been accepted in America. The phenomenon is a familiar one in all other domestic animals, such as dogs, pigs, goats, sheep, rabbits, etc. Further experimental breeding very soon proved that this mutation of hang-ears is dominant. Geneticists in the United Kingdom have recorded precise data over five generations. It was noted that this characteristic does not develop fully until the animal is a little more than three months old. Vision and hearing remain normal. There are now several different colour varieties of hang-eared cats in England and Scotland. In 1971 a breeding line was established in the Federal Republic of Germany.

Hairless cats are a further case of hereditary abnormality. This form of total hairlessness is well known in other domestic animals, for example, in dogs and laboratory mice and rats. This phenomenon can appear in all kinds of cat breeds. It is a case of loss-mutation, a degeneration, whereby the ability to produce a coat of hair has been lost. Only the whiskers are retained.

In Canada, hairless Siamese cats were recognised as a breed under the name of Sphinx cat. The aesthetic considerations usually applied to cat beauty remain extremely doubtful in this instance. Moreover, these wrinkled, bare-skinned creatures, whose skin lacks natural insulation against heat loss, are exceptionally weak and delicate, and their hairlessness also seems to be linked with mortality or partial mortality factors.

Rex cats

The Rex first appeared in Cornwall in 1950, in the litter of a short-haired farm cat. It is a mutation, a sudden genetic change, which manifested itself in the form of a certain condition of the coat, hitherto unknown in cats. As in the Rex rabbit, the coat is curly. This first Rex tom founded the line of Cornish Rex, the English mutation. In 1951, a Rex cat was bred in Berlin. In the course of subsequent breeding in France, it was termed 'German Rex'. In the late 'fifties, a further specimen with a curly coat appeared in the USA, the 'Oregon Rex'. In 1960, a second one appeared in Devon, and was named 'Devon Rex'.

Since the first Rex cats differed from other short-haired cats only in the condition of their coat, there was initially some reluctance to accept them as a separate breed, but to regard them only as a coat variation. The curly coat could in fact occur equally in a Siamese, a longhair or in other breeds. It would simply have been a matter of adding 'Rex' to whichever existing standard they corresponded to. However, this was not what happened.

With its wavy, or curly-haired coat, the outward appearance of the Rex cat differs from that of a normal-coated cat, even the whiskers being crinkled. The composition of the coat is not, however, instantly recognisable as different. The normal coat of a cat consists of the fine, short, down-hairs of the under-fur, the awn hairs of the over-fur and the outer, straight guard hairs. The Cornish, German and Oregon Rex all have only one thick coat of down-hairs, with occasional guard hairs, while some Cornish Rex have only woolly hairs, making the coat particularly soft and fine. The Devon Rex supposedly possess all three types of hair, but they are more brittle, break easily and are very sparsely distributed.

Hairless, or partially hairless cats also occur within the Rex breed. However, since hairlessness is linked with a mortality factor, these cats should not be used for breeding.

Genetically, the tendency to wavy hair is recessive to normal coat condition. Thus a pure Rex litter can only be expected if both parents are genotypically identical. A cross between a Cornish Rex and a Devon Rex produced a normal, straight-coated litter. By contrast, a German or Oregon Rex crossed with a Cornish Rex produced only Rex-coated kittens. This proves that there must be two different Rex-mutation strains.

The offspring of Cornish Rex, German Rex and Oregon Rex are therefore classified as Gen 1 Rex under standard No. 33, while those of the Devon Rex are Gen 2 Rex under No. 33 a.

The two mutants differ in type. The Cornish, German and Oregon Rex are rather more stockily built, and have a loose, wavy coat. The Devon Rex are distinctly slender animals with whiplash tails, narrow heads, slanting eyes and enormous ears. Many Devon Rex cats only have down on their underparts. This should not be mistaken for hairlessness.

Two further mutant types have been developed in America. One is the Peke-faced longhair, which has a brachycephalic, pushed-in face like that of Pekinese and Pug dogs. As with those dogs this can lead to breathing difficulties, blocked tear ducts and problems in jaw alignment, which place an enormous onus on breeders to avoid perpetuating deformities. Concern both for the animal's health and for preserving the basic feline look have prevented the breed being taken up on the other side of the Atlantic and it is not recognised in either Britain or Europe.

Another, even stranger cat, is the Ragdoll, a mutation occurring in the kittens of a cat which had been severely injured in an accident. This breed hangs limp, like a ragdoll or beanbag lying over the arm, and seems to have little sense of either danger or pain. It has to be carefully looked after to ensure that no harm befalls it but has found an appeal with people who want a cat which is, as their breeder puts it, 'the closest one can get to a real live baby and have an animal'. It may not appeal so much to anyone who wants a cat.

Matthew Arnold Matthias and Atossa

Poor Matthias! Would'st thou have
More than pity? claim'st a stave?
—Friends more near us than a bird
We dismissed without a word,
Rover, with the good brown head,
Great Atossa, they are dead;
Dead, and neither prose nor rhyme
Tells the praises of their prime.
Thou did'st know them old and grey,
Knew them in their sad decay.
Thou hast seen Atossa sage
Sit for hours beside thy cage;

Thou would'st chirp, thou foolish bird,
Flutter, chirp—she never stir'd!
What were now these toys to her?
Down she sank amid her fur;
Eyed thee with a soul resign'd—
And thou deemedst cats were kind!
—Cruel, but composed and bland,
Dumb, inscrutable and grand,
So Tiberius might have sat,
Had Tiberius been a cat.

The chief identifiable feature of the cat, including the domestic cat, is its characteristic teeth. The kitten begins to produce its milk teeth at between four and five weeks, and these are complete by the age of eight weeks. The change from milk teeth to permanent dentition takes place at some time between four and six months. The cat's adult teeth number 30. Both the upper and lower jaw each have six sharp incisors, and two fangs. Next to the fangs, the cat has four molars on each side of the upper jaw, but only three on each side of the lower jaw. Each of the third molars in the upper and lower jaw is very well developed and serves as a scissor tooth. The location of the scissor teeth means that food for biting is pushed right to the back of the corner of the mouth. The head is turned down to the side with which the cat is chewing. Since both masticatory muscles are weak, the cat will frequently change sides while chewing. Indeed, it often requires several changes from side to side, before a single morsel is bitten off, and swallowed, usually accompanied by a jerking movement of the head. In between the cat has to keep licking its mouth and nose.

Fragments of meat are detached from a bone with the incisors, but also may be rasped off with the rough tongue. The tongue is densely covered with extremely powerful papillae that slope backwards and act like a grater. The front incisors are small, and consequently inadequate for biting off normal, bite-sized pieces. As indicated earlier, the back part of the dentition is constructed for biting, but cats frequently tear off pieces and swallow them whole, without chewing.

If the cat is not very hungry and is not disturbed while feeding, it will eat slowly and without any show of greediness. It will pause frequently to clean itself in between eating.

Like most animals, cats have an alimentary tract extending three to five times their body length. The stomach secretes acidic gastric juices, so that the bones of the smaller animals caught and eaten by the predatory cat are easily digested. Peristol and peristalsis ensure the thorough mixing and transport of the ingested food.

The cat's diet

A mixed feeder
with a predator's teeth

90

Nutrients *Carbohydrates* All the ingredients necessary for building up and maintaining the cat's body should be included in its diet. Carbohydrates form one of the major constituents of the diet for they supply the body with the energy to maintain all its vital functions. They occur in the form of starch and sugars. The organism converts carbohydrates into fats and amino-acids. Carbohydrates are present in all cereals and vegetable matter but cats cannot handle very much starch and roughage and these should be cooked to facilitate the digestion and absorption of the food. Creamed rice is often fed to kittens and some cats will eat breakfast cereals. Proprietary foods often contain a proportion of cereal. Cats are much more difficult in the green vegetables they accept and this will vary from individual to individual and they may refuse all except grass.

Protein Another important basic food is protein. Amino-acids are the nitrogenous components of all proteins. To date more than 30 of them are known to science. Approximately 12 of these are either vital or essential. These basic ingredients of proteins, the essential amino-acids, must be included in a biologically balanced diet. Cats will obtain all the protein that they need from their normal diet of cooked or raw meat and fish and, unless they are underfed, are unlikely to suffer from a protein deficiency. Additional protein can be obtained from eggs and vegetable protein.

Fats Fats are a third important component of the diet. Fat serves to build up the body and at the same time produces energy, which we measure in terms of calories, for all the bodily functions. The high energy value of fats makes them into important reserves in the body. The bodies of animals keep fat deposits in special storage networks, so that if at any time their normal energy requirements cannot be satisfied through normal food intake, these reserves can be mobilised. However, to conclude from this that it is desirable to build up a hefty cushion of fat in a little kitten would be fundamentally wrong. The same applies to other mammals as to humans: always maintain a happy medium. Only hibernating mammals, such as the bear, or camels crossing long stretches of desert or the fat-tail sheep or goat of the Middle East need to lay down large deposits of fat. Unsaturated, fatty acids which are concerned in the breakdown and building up of body fat, are absolutely indispensable. These fatty acids must be present in the animal's food. They are a stage in the conversion of carbohydrates into fats, and it is in this form that fats are absorbed from the intestine. Moreover, fats are the vehicle of the fat-soluble Vitamins A, D, E and K and are essential for the animal's resistance to infection. However, not every fat is suitable for inclusion in the diet. In no case should one act according to the totally wrong principle: 'What is no longer fit for man, is still good enough to give the animals.' Do not feed your cat food that has been kept too long.

Mineral salts, vitamins, roughage If every trace of water is extracted from food, the resulting dry substance will consist of organic matter, such as proteins, fats, carbohydrates and vitamins, and of inorganic matter or mineral salts. The mineral salts that appear in considerable quantities are calcium, sodium, phosphorus, potassium, magnesium, sulphur and chlorine. In addition there are the trace elements, for example, iron, manganese, copper, cobalt, zinc, iodine and fluoride. Both groups of elements are vital, since deficiency in any one of these will prevent the animal from thriving. They are of great importance as blood constituents, and as essential ingredients that have a complex relationship to hormones, enzymes and vitamins. The mineral requirement is particularly high where the body has to meet additional demands such as during extreme physical exertion or during growth, convalescence, pregnancy and similar conditions.

Vitamins are essential and reach the body either naturally, in food, or as an added supplement, but also through the activity of certain microorganisms in the digestive tract. Vitamins fulfil certain vital tasks in the body and are physiologically highly active. Since, apart from Vitamin A, vitamins cannot be stored in the body, a constant supply of them is necessary. Absence of vitamins is called avitaminosis, and insufficiency of vitamins, hypovitaminosis. However, excess of certain vitamins can also be harmful, and lead to symptoms of hypervitaminosis. Severe neglect and malnutrition produce vitamin deficiency illnesses. Such severe disturbances of the metabolism, however, seldom occur in cats. A vitamin excess can sometimes be as damaging as a deficiency, too much Vitamin A, for instance, causing an overgrowth of bones in the neck.

An incorrect mineral balance due to a shortage of calcium or of phosphates may result in incomplete development of the bone tissue, a condition which is sometimes seen in young cats, most frequently in Siamese. This is known as 'osteodystrophy', which may involve an hereditary susceptibility. Curvature of the legs and motor difficulties, and also predisposition to fractures, are indications of such diseases. Rickets is directly due to a calcium/phosphate imbalance or deficiency. (See the chapter concerned with illnesses.) Raising the mineral intake and treatment with doses of Vitamins A, B_1, B_{12}, D and E are urgently indicated. Immediate change of diet to varied, nutritious food is essential. Hypovitaminoses are, however, by far the most frequent, and can, for example, take the form of poor growth, lack of appetite and lowered resistance to infectious diseases.

Roughage is the undigestible part of the diet, which different animal species require in very varying amounts. Roughage promotes active peristalsis and induces regular stomach function and digestion.

Animals in the wild instinctively seek out the active substances they require. Animal owners must always take care to provide their charges with food of the best quality. It is very difficult to pinpoint where a deficiency occurs in the diet—whether it is vitamins, trace elements or mineral salts. As a rule, there is more than one deficiency. Yet in practice it is rare for any vitamin, trace element or mineral salt to be entirely absent from a diet. It is usually a matter of insufficiency or too much fluctuation in the content. Above all, it should be borne in mind that the needs of the cat change according to its age, weight, condition and the time of year. A cat's requirements always increase if it is either pregnant or suckling kittens. Once signs of deficiency become evident, they have already reached an advanced stage, that is to say, the deficiency has existed for a long period, and all available body reserves have been exhausted. This kind of imbalance may exist for weeks, months and even years, without the owner being aware of it. An impoverished diet causes emaciation, whereas insufficient vitamins and trace elements lead to functional disorders. Insufficient trace elements or vitamins will in any case make an animal more prone to sickness than protein deficiency. It is essentially a matter of keeping the right balance between all the different ingredients of the diet.

Table 1: Vitamins and their meaning

Vitamins	Main function	Symptoms of deficiency	Source of vitamin
Fat-soluble vitamins			
Vitamin A (and provitamin = carotene)	growth promotion; protection of the epithelia, e.g. skin	reduction of growth, loss of sight, lesions of the mucous membrane	milk, eggs, cod-liver oil, liver, dried yeast, Vitamin A concentrate
Vitamin D (and provitamins D_2 and D_3)	regulation of the calcium-phosphorus relation, bone formation	rickets in young cats; bone brittleness in older animals; growth or reproductive disorders	cod-liver oil, yeast, fish liver, fresh eggs, fresh air and sunshine, (danger of excess)
Vitamin E	regulation of reproductive functions, control of hormone reserves and carbohydrate assimilation	sexual malfunction, sterility, abortion; heart damage	corn, milk, vegetables
Vitamin K (cats manufacture this vitamin in the intestine)	formation of blood-clotting enzymes	delay in blood clotting, appearance/signs of muscular and skin bleeding	cod-liver oil, liver, fish meal, vegetables, synthesis of intestinal bacetria
Water-soluble vitamins			
Vitamin B Complex	regulation of metabolism; enzyme formation, formation of blood	B_1: nervous disorders, oedemas, convulsions B_2: diarrhoea, arrested development B_6: skin diseases, anaemia, convulsions *Nicotinic acid*: emaciation, skin defects, diarrhoea *Pantothenic acid*: skin inflammation, liver damage *Folic acid*: anaemia, arrested development/inhibited growth B_{12}: anaemia and inhibited growth	synthesis of intestinal bacteria, milk, yeast, cod-liver oil, liver meal, meat and fish meal, animal protein, green vegetables, corn
Vitamin C	activating enzymes and hormones	scurvy, with loss of teeth, reduced bone growth	greens, vegetables, fruit, milk, raw meat, liver, kidneys

Here, too, the first and foremost principle to keep in mind is that the cat is an individualist! Where feeding the house or pedigree cat is concerned, it is hard to put forward firm rules or recipes. Each cat will want to be treated as an individual, and each cat has its own particular fads and fancies.

Yet, in order to keep our charge healthy, we are obliged to introduce certain principles and consistently observe them.

The view that a mouse-catching cat does not need to be fed, is long out-dated. Only a strong, healthy—that is well-fed—house cat is able to engage in productive mouse-hunting. Small mammals such as mice are, moreover, often not just potential food for the cat, but more a hunting target.

Regularity Whether the cat is a pet or pedigree, what it wants above all else is to receive its food regularly and punctually. All animals will adapt with extraordinary speed to externally imposed, regular, rhythmic occurrences, since in the course of its own natural life-span it likewise submits to similar rhythms, the so-called 'internal clock'.

Whereas small kittens, or sick and feeble cats and cats in the process of changing from milk to adult teeth, may prefer meat that has been minced or finely chopped, the healthy, adult cat should be given pieces of meat, the size of a nut. This is not to say that it would be wrong to feed the cat occasionally on larger, possibly tenderised meat rissoles, or even a piece of meat on the bone, so that it can spend longer in eating it. Using its rough tongue it will rasp the last shreds of meat from the bone. Chewing meat rissoles involves a healthy form of massage that is necessary every now and again in order to strengthen the muscles used for mastication.

As a rule, cats take their time over eating. Unlike a pack animal such as the dog, the cat does not appear to have a pronounced love of food. Some cats will take every scrap of meat out of the dish in turn and eat it from the floor. Only where several cats are kept together need care be taken that the animals do not compete with each other for food. Once this happens, they will all rush at once at the food, amidst scuffing, hissing and spitting, and the scraps of food will be bolted indiscriminately. In such a case, the only thing to do is to feed the animals separately, until harmony and order are restored. Admittedly such behaviour can also be exploited to advantage. The presence of a rival feeder will soon cause a finicky kitten to improve its poor feeding habits.

Freshness of the food Mushy food seems less attractive to some cats than a firm meal. Perhaps this is because they are so fastidious and after a mushy meal the grooming of nose and fur, which invariably follows eating, will inevitably take much longer.

All food should be fresh and uncontaminated. Preferably food should always be served at room temperature, if not at body heat, since this comes closest to natural conditions. At any rate, food should never be given straight from the refrigerator. This is a mistake that is always being made with milk. A hungry cat waiting to snatch a particular delicacy may try to take food that is too hot, so let it cool to a reasonable temperature. Obviously, the cat's feeding dish should be thoroughly washed every time, before being filled with food. The cat will almost invariably leave left-overs untouched. Even when extremely hungry, it will seldom eat stale food.

94

A cat fed a well-balanced diet does not normally require supplements, but dietary needs do vary, a kitten needing calcium for instance to build strong bones and pregnant cats needing suitable mineral and vitamin supplements.

Dishes prepared for human consumption need not necessarily be rejected out of hand as unsuitable for the house or pedigree cat, but one should consider carefully whether they will, in fact, agree with the cat. Human fare is sometimes excessively fatty. Cats, however, often like highly-seasoned food.

Number of meals   There are no hard and fast rules as to the number of meals to give a cat. Careful observation of the cat will soon indicate the right amount. Always remember that a slender but active cat is far more natural and healthy than a plump and lazy cat.

Overfeeding causes obesity, reduces resistance to disease and consequently shortens the life-span of the cat considerably. Depending on the particular circumstances and the condition of the animal, the following figures may be taken as a rough guide: kittens up to three months old benefit from up to four feeds per day, three to five months, two to three feeds, and five to nine months, two feeds will suffice. Normally, a fully-grown cat will need feeding only morning and evening, and in most cases, one meal a day is quite adequate.

There is scarcely any wild animal that, in the wild, catches prey every day. It is a common practice in zoos that, every so often, beasts of prey are made to fast for a day—a principle that could be recommended for the domestic cat, and is already adopted by many breeders. If an otherwise healthy cat does not appear to be hungry and tries only to tease out the favourite titbits from its food, it can quite safely be left to go hungry for a day or even longer. Cats can last out for days before they will touch food of which they are not particularly fond. In such a case, it is best to be hard-hearted, and not to give in.

Composition of the diet   Once again, it is worth pointing out that a poor diet may equally be due to the wrong quantity as to the wrong quality. Too much feeding can be just as harmful as too little.

All cats, and long-haired cats in particular, need fresh grass from time to time, in order to clean out the gastro-intestinal tract. The grass often makes the cat vomit and in so doing helps it bring up hairs that it has swallowed in the course of cleaning itself. Preventing the cat from doing this, will eventually lead to the formation of the dreaded hair balls, which can cause constipation, inflammation of the gastro-intestinal tract and worse. In cases of extreme need, the cat will even be driven to nibbling at the most diverse indoor plants.

If the cat cannot be allowed out of doors daily, to where growing grass is available, a clean clump of grass should occasionally be dug up and placed near its feeding dish. Better still grow a pot of grass and have a fresh supply indoors. Pots of commercially prepared growing medium, already planted with grass seed, are available which rapidly germinate after watering. They need to be kept damp. If your cat pulls at them too violently or eats too rapidly they should be placed out of reach to enable the grass to recover and grow again.

95

A varied, mixed and versatile diet is important for the health of a cat. Why, in fact, a mixed diet for an animal that is naturally a carnivore?

Meat Most meat and meat offals are suitable for cats, although individuals may show particular preferences. Carcass meat fed as the sole diet may result in calcium, iodine and Vitamin A deficiencies. Opinions vary as to whether meat should be given raw or cooked. Pork, which can carry tapeworm should be cooked but provided always that it be fresh and the cat shows no preference the choice is yours—but do not serve meat still chilled from the refrigerator. As far as offal is concerned, liver, kidneys, lungs, heart and brains are all suitable, and liver and blood in particular are rich in iron. Liver has the highest vitamin content, and is an especially important source of Vitamins A, D, C and B Complex. Raw liver, however, has a laxative effect and should not be served in excessive quantities.

A diet limited to any one particular type of food could lead to health damage. Liver, for instance, is rich in Vitamin A and a persistently excessive intake of this vitamin can result in marked changes in the skeleton. With young cats the transformation of cartilage into bone is seriously impaired, bone growth is severely inhibited and firm bony tissue softens. In adult cats it leads to stiffening of the vertebral joints. Inertia, lameness and apathy are often the first warning signs. Raw liver should then be given only as an occasional treat and in no more than the appropriate quantity. If a surplus makes it necessary to use it, it can be braised or boiled, the vitamin content thereby being considerably reduced. If, however, the vitamin content needs to be increased, belly of beef can also be given. Offal discarded in butchering and fish processing is used to manufacture valuable meat and fish meal. Fish meal, for example, contains 61.8 per cent raw protein and 8.6 per cent raw fat. Meat meal contains 66 per cent raw protein and 10.5 per cent raw fat. The mineral salt content of bone meal makes it an excellent food. Blood meal is a pure protein food. Cod-liver oil, so important and so often referred to, is made from the liver of cod, shark and tuna fish. Its value lies in its high content of Vitamins A and D.

With their high protein and vitamin content, eggs are a valuable part of the diet. The predominant mineral salts present in eggs are phosphorus, calcium and iron.

Veal cartilage, bones that have not yet hardened, are a favourite. They are not so much a food, as a source of mineral salts and also help to strengthen the cat's teeth.

Rabbit meat is highly nutritious, easily digested and low in fat, and is particularly suitable for raising young animals and as invalid fare. The same goes for poultry, which

96

can also be used if the animal has been put on a diet, as the meat is tender and mostly low in fat. Great care must be taken with the bones, however, as they are sharp and fragments can easily cause dangerous injuries in the gastro-intestinal tract. The rather tough, firm skin is often rejected and for safety's sake is best removed.

Fish, milk, vegetables, puddings   Fish, either raw, cooked or smoked is very eagerly taken, and should certainly be given for variety's sake, provided certain precautions are observed. A totally fish diet should be avoided, in some cases it may cause or aggravate a form of eczema. Except for very small fish it is probably safer to bone and cook fish rather than expect the cat to fillet them itself.

Creamy milk is highly nutritious, containing all the basic essential nutritive substances. It is of primary importance in the raising of young cats. Nevertheless some caution is advisible when giving it to cats, some have difficulty in digesting milk, and it may cause diarrhoea. Orientals may reject it completely when past kittenhood. Cow's milk consists of 3.5 to 4 per cent fat, 3.2 per cent protein, 4.7 per cent lactose, 0.7 per cent ash and 83 per cent water. Cream cheese or curd cheese is enjoyed by some cats and may be given as a treat.

Some cats enjoy eating vegetables with often quite eccentric preferences, they should be lightly cooked to aid digestion. Pasta (noodles, spaghetti, etc.), boiled potatoes and pulses (lentils, barley, etc), porridge oats and rice moistened with unseasoned meat broth are foods rich in carbohydrates, which help to vary the diet, provided they are not included in too great quantities. Of course, not all cats will accept them. Further variety can be achieved by using the many different commercially available proprietary cat foods in tins, moist and dried forms (see p. 98f.). A mixture of fresh and commercially prepared foods is probably the ideal diet providing the maximum nutritional value.

The cat's drinking needs   The cat's tongue is its most important and indispensable implement for taking in fluid. Cats are unable to sip a drink simply by sucking it in. The liquid has to be lapped up in a series of rapid movements by a spoon-like curving of the tongue. The hook-shaped papillae that densely cover the upper part of the tongue, to some extent help the fluid on its way down into the throat.

The cat should always be given water to drink. Milk is a liquid food, especially valuable for pregnant or nursing cats, but even if you are giving the cat milk, you should always provide water as well, to quench its thirst. Many cats refuse to drink milk. At certain times, even the cat accustomed to milk will only drink water. As milk very quickly turns sour in hot weather or in warm homes, only put as much out for a cat as it can drink in one go. Normally, water and milk should be warmed to room temperature. In no case take milk from the refrigerator and pour it straight into the cat's dish. This may cause intestinal shock.

Some young cats will not take ordinary milk, but love tinned milk. In this case, select evaporated (not condensed) tinned milk that is low in fat content. Older cats may occasionally be allowed tinned milk containing more fat, but it should be diluted in proportions of two-thirds milk to one-third water, and should always be given lukewarm.

Nowadays there is a constant increase in the use of convenience foods. The production of commercial pet foods is now a multi-million pound business. When people realise how much is spent on pets and what a large amount of food they eat in a world where so many human beings live in poverty and are starving they may question whether pet owners have their priorities right. However, our pets play an important role in ameliorating some of the strains and problems of modern life and it is doubtful whether depriving people of their pets would actually lead to any benefits for needy humans. Much of the meat used in pet foods is in forms which would not find a sale as human food.

Commercial cat foods

Most of the conveniently packaged cat foods available in Britain and North America are produced by big companies that have their own research laboratories and carry out extensive nutritional studies. They have formulated cat foods which provide a balanced diet incorporating the vitamin and mineral supplements that provide a cat with all its nutritional needs. Cans and packages are usually labelled to indicate the composition of the contents and you will be able to see the constituents, which will usually include meat or fish, cereals, vegetable protein and additional supplements. Whale meat was once the basis of many pet foods until fear for the remaining whale population and pressure from the movement for their protection turned public opinion against the practice in some countries.

It could be claimed that a cat fed solely on canned cat food produced to a well-formulated recipe has a better diet than many cats fed on fresh meat but which lack some of the essential trace elements, vitamins and minerals. However, most cats will enjoy tearing at fresh meat and exercising their teeth and jaws on the occasional firm raw bone. (Never risk serving cats brittle, soft or sharp-pointed bones.)

Commercial cat foods are now available in three main types: canned, dried and moist. All are packaged to keep well for long periods in the store-cupboard.

Canned foods have been established longer than the other types and are still the most popular. Purchase them in sizes which give you sufficient for only one day's feeding so that you offer fresh food each day and do not allow it to become contaminated. Cats will often show a marked preference for a particular brand or flavour—not necessarily the most expensive—but it would be wise to vary what you offer so that your cat does not become too set in its ways. Some canned foods have a rather mushy texture which certain cats may reject; others have a more chunky texture. Many brands offer a range of flavour types as variations to a basic recipe.

98

Moist foods are sold in airtight sachets. They are usually shaped into small cubes or balls and some of the moisture has been extracted from them to give a firm texture. Packages usually contain a number of sachets, each of which is sufficient for one cat's daily needs. After serving a portion the opening of the foil bag can be folded over to keep the contents fresh until the next mealtime. Since these foods have a reduced moisture content cats will need to drink more water to accompany them.

Dried foods will usually keep for some time after opening the pack, provided that they are stored in a dry place. Naturally if there is any sign of them developing mould they should not be given to the cat. When dried foods were first introduced there was some controversy over the possibility that they might lead to a painful urinary condition in cats. A change in formula reduced the risk but cat urine is very concentrated and the development of bladder stones or of 'sand' that blocks the urethra, particularly of the male, is not uncommon if cats do not take much liquid. Since the removal of the moisture from these foods reduces a cat's liquid intake considerably it is essential that cats fed upon them drink plenty of water. If a cat tends not to drink very much it would be safer not to offer it dried foods. However, many cats find them particularly attractive and crunching them probably helps keep the teeth healthy. An alternative way of serving these foods is to pour water (or stock) over them so that they absorb it and the moisture content is maintained.

Some cats enjoy the biscuits and biscuit meal produced for dogs and you may be able to obtain similar biscuits specially formulated for cats. They may be served dry or soaked in milk, gravy or water.

Some foods, fish especially, are marketed for cats in frozen form (often it comes packaged to boil in the bag). It should be cooked in the same way as for human consumption and never offered in its frozen state.

Dehydrated meat is also sometimes available for cats. It should be reconstituted in the same way as similar human foods.

Always check the composition of the commercial foods that you offer your cat. Buying the most expensive will not guarantee it the most balanced diet, for an expensive can of meat and gravy will require balancing with carbohydrates and vitamins, which may already be incorporated in a cheaper recipe that does not offer so much concentrated meat.

Feeding kittens and adult cats

Having established the most essential foods for a healthy diet, we should now like to go into greater detail on how to draw up a well-balanced diet sheet.

Quantities   Let us assume that as a rule the cat has one to two feeds a day. Fully-grown cats require approximately 100–200g ($3\frac{1}{2}$–7 oz) of food per day. As a rough guide you can reckon 15g per kilogramme of body weight ($\frac{1}{2}$ oz per lb) daily is sufficient, although cats that are overweight should, of course, be fed less. If the diet is based on a healthy mixture of raw animal and vegetable fare together with some commercial complete food, this would mean that approximately 50–100 g ($1\frac{3}{4}$–$3\frac{1}{2}$ oz) of muscle meat or any offal such as liver, lung, kidneys, brains, or fish or poultry with approximately the same amount of ready-prepared food, plus a corresponding supplement of one tablespoon of any kind of vegetable would provide a good meal for most cats. Variations on this formula should be made throughout the week. If no ready-prepared food is available, substitute a corresponding amount of cooked meat, pasta or cereal, or something similar. The amount depends on the cat's appetite, temperament and current condition, and will vary accordingly. A pregnant or nursing cat, in particular, requires a more substantial diet and larger quantities, and should be offered food four to five times a day. At such times calcium, mineral and vitamin supplements should be included. Plenty of fresh water must always be available. Animals that get little exercise, should have correspondingly less food. The amount of food should be very carefully estimated, and be only just so much that the cat devours it hungrily without leaving anything. There should be no left-overs on a cat's dish.

In principle, kittens should be fed the same as cats, but less at a time and more often. However there are a number of minor details that need closer observation.

Supplementary feeding Depending on the health of the kittens, the size of the litter and the physical condition of the mother, kittens can be fed their first supplementary food at between three and four weeks. If the mother still has milk—and this is normally the case up to the age of nine to ten weeks—then supplementary feeding is adequate. Otherwise, the kitten should be given full meals. For a normal supplement, some creamed rice, boned chicken or fish and evaporated milk given twice daily, at morning and evening, is quite adequate. Kittens will probably also show an interest in their mother's food. Kittens will sometimes start feeding themselves by the age of three weeks and may be entirely weaned at six to seven weeks, although most will still take the opportunity of suckling. Except in the case of orphan kittens or litters too large for a cat to raise (see the chapter on hand-rearing), feeding bottles should not be used but food should be offered in a saucer or feeding bowl. If a kitten is slow to lap and take solid food dab a little milk or creamed rice on its nose. Usually it will eagerly lick this off and the transition to eating will be quickly made. Gradually the meat and fish content of the diet can be increased. Once a kitten has got its teeth the occasional portion of dried food may be offered. Egg-yolk, a half teaspoonful of glucose and a few drops of cod-liver oil may also be given from time to time.

As the kittens show an increasing demand for solid food increase the number of meals rather than the quantity at each, for kittens have very small stomachs and gorging themselves may cause problems.

Kittens should in no circumstances be taken to their new homes at less than eight weeks old. Even then, a detailed feeding plan should be handed over with them, to avoid further stress resulting from a change of diet at what is already a difficult time caused by separation from their mother, change of owner and acclimatisation to a new home. Suggestions as to methods of feeding can also be most helpful to the new owner. However, no form of food can fully replace the mother's milk. No kitten should be taken from its mother until it is fully weaned, unless it is absolutely essential because of sickness or to prevent undue strain on the mother.

70 *The cat's large canine teeth are designed to catch and hold its prey. This Cream longhair probably does little hunting but that does not impair the effectiveness of its teeth.*

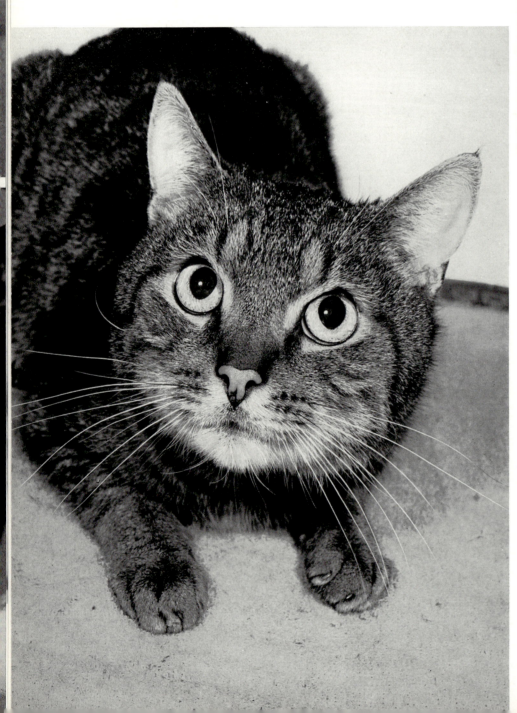

74/75/76/77   *Portraits of mongrel pets*

71/72 *If you serve food at regular times most cats will turn up promptly. Even feral cats quickly learn the timetable of food provided for them.*

73 *This cat has its own improvised lift service to enable it to enjoy an outdoor life. It returns when called to be hauled back to its home upstairs.*

Table 2: Diet for kittens	1st week: (hand-reared kittens)	every 2 hours	1 tsp unsweetened, undiluted evaporated milk or powdered milk substitute for mother's milk, such as Lactol, as recommended by manufacturer
	2nd week: hand-reared kittens)	day: every 2 hours, night: every 3 hours	1 large tin evaporated milk beaten up with 1 egg-yolk. Give 1 tsp of this for each feed
	3rd week: (hand-reared kittens)	omit 1 feed per day and increase portions	as 2nd week
	4th–5th week: (hand-reared kittens, smaller quantities if being weaned)	6–7 meals per day, omit night feeds	Add cooked cereal and pea-sized pieces of chicken, rabbit or scraped beef. Gradually increase quantities. Milk and meat. Serve in dish
	6th–12th week:	4 meals daily	*morning*: $\frac{1}{6}$ cup egg-milk-cereal mixture. 2 tbs raw meat *noon*: $\frac{1}{6}$ cup egg-milk-cereal mixture *evening*: 2 tbs meat or fish, and 1 tsp cooked vegetable *late evening*: $\frac{1}{6}$ cup egg-milk-cereal mixture, 2 tbs meat or fish
	12th–16th week:	3 meals daily	*morning*: 2 tbs egg-milk-cereal mixture *noon*: 2 tbs scraped meat (raw beef), or kidney cut up fine. 2 tbs egg-milk-cereal mixture *late evening*: 2 tbs egg-milk-cereal mixture. Gradually increase portions, ending up $1\frac{1}{2}$ times more. Always give water. (Some owners add a little crusted garlic to the occasional meal, believing this to help prevent worms. There is no scientific proof that it does but many cats like the taste of garlic and of onions.)
	16th–20th week:	2 meals daily	*morning*: $\frac{1}{3}-\frac{1}{4}$ cup egg-milk-cereal mixture. 2 tbs meat (or heart, liver, lung, kidney, brains) *evening*: 4 tbs meat with 1 tsp cereal and vegetable (also fish), 2 tbs meat
	20th–24th week: (at this age cats will often accept being fed only once per day)	2 meals daily	approx. 150–200 g ($5\frac{1}{4}$–7 oz) meat, fish or offal, with cereal and vegetables, daily

109

Two cats at night by Joseph Hegenbarth

Christopher Smart # To My Cat Jeoffrey

For I will consider my cat Jeoffrey.

For he is the servant of the Living God, duly and daily serving him ...

For first he looks upon his fore-paws to see if they are clean.

For secondly he kicks up behind to clear away there.

For thirdly he works it upon stretch with the fore-paws extended.

For fourthly he sharpens his paws by wood.

For fifthly he washes himself.

For sixthly he rolls upon wash.

For seventhly he fleas himself, that he may not be interrupted upon the beat.

For eighthly he rubs himself against a post.

For ninthly he looks up for his instructions.

For tenthly he goes in quest of food.

For having considered God and himself he will consider his neighbour.

For if he meets another cat he will kiss her in kindness.

For when he takes his prey he plays with it to give it chance.

For one mouse in seven escapes by his dallying.

For when his day's work is done his business more properly begins.

For he keeps the Lord's watch in the night against the adversary.

For he counteracts the powers of darkness by his electrical skin and glaring eyes.

For he counteracts the Devil, who is death, by brisking about the life.

For in his morning orisons he loves the sun and the sun loves him.

For he is of the tribe of Tiger.

For the Cherub Cat is a term of the Angel Tiger.

For he has the subtlety and hissing of a serpent, which in goodness he suppresses.

For he will not do destruction if he is well-fed, neither will he spit without provocation.

For he purrs in thankfulness, when God tells him he's a good Cat.

Long-haired cats

Uncertainty surrounds the origin of long-haired cats. It is likely that a longhair mutation could not have survived until after cats had become domesticated and the first evidence of domestic cats with long hair comes from the Middle East. From Turkey and Persia travellers brought back tales of long-haired cats and as early as 1521 the cats themselves were being taken back to Italy from Khorasan in Persia.

Although the name Persian was used to cover most longhairs (and still is by most American cat fanciers) until the GCCF decided that longhair should be the official term, the cat which first became established in Europe was more probably a Turkish cat, which we know as the Angora, and which has been saved from extinction in recent times by a special breeding programme at Ankara Zoo. The name is a corruption of that of the Turkish capital. This is a slimmer cat than the Persian type, with a smaller head and longer body. Its fur is like that of the Angora rabbit or the Turkish Angora goat which gives us mohair. Some of the cats from Ankara Zoo have been taken to America and the breed has become established there but it is still not recognised in Britain and Europe.

The British do, however, recognise another Turkish cat which is of similar conformation to the Angora. At first known as the Van cat, and now officially as the Turkish cat, it has an auburn tail and auburn markings on the face. It comes from the area of Lake Van in Turkey and has a reputation for enjoying the occasional swim.

111

During the last century interest shifted to the Persian type of longhair and it is this which has been developed into a whole range of long-haired breeds. They are truly creatures of luxury that can only exist under the protective care of man. Their compact body with comparatively short legs, shows off the long hair to best advantage. The round, wide head, with large, round eyes, again suits it well. The snub-nose, the so-called Persian stop, unfortunately frequently causes the eyes to water. Their behaviour is also quite different from that of short-haired cats. They are considerably more placid, gentle and reflective. They do, however, require a great deal more attention, because the coat needs so much care. They are not much suited to a tough life out of doors.

Today's long-haired cats have the same kind of colouring as short-haired cats. Thus there are the Black longhair with copper-coloured eyes, White with blue, orange or odd-coloured eyes; Blue, Red, Cream, Bi-colour, Smoke and Red and Brown tabbies, all with deep copper eyes. Then there are Silver tabbies with green or hazel eyes, the green-eyed Chinchilla, the Tortoiseshell, with distinct patches of black, red and cream, the Tortoiseshell and white, with well-defined patches of black, red and cream, interspersed with white, the Blue-cream, and finally the Siamese-coloured Colourpoints and Birmans with brilliant blue eyes, which will be discussed in the chapter on breeds of mixed origin.

With blue-eyed white longhairs there is the danger of deafness, since the blue eye-colour factor is coupled with another genetic factor which inhibits the normal development of the inner ear.

Kittens born with a dark patch in their fur, which fades as they mature, rarely prove to be deaf. When testing a cat for deafness, it is important not to let the cat *see* the cause of the noise or to detect an oscillation by its sense of touch.

It is worth noting that with Black longhairs, the kittens are often a very poor colour. The coat sometimes remains grey up to five or six months, or is stippled with white or even rust-coloured hairs. These will often turn black as the animals reach adulthood. Breeding Black longhairs is not simple. If the hair is too soft, these animals will always appear brownish in colour. Only the firmer hair produces the lustrous gloss and pitch-

A Smoke longhair

black colouring. The best blacks are the product of Blue with Black. Breeding White with Black can sometimes be successful, too. With White longhairs, the kittens sometimes have a grey or black patch on the head, which disappears as they grow older. In adult animals yellowish stripes, which are caused by the sebaceous glands, often appear on the tail. Since these are considered a fault in shows, watch out for them, and clean them off beforehand.

The Chinchilla kitten, at birth, seems very dark and will usually show tabby markings on the face. The legs, too, have shadow stripes. After about 14 days, these markings on the legs darken, and recede from the face. The coat does not lighten until between three and four months, when the silver ruff begins to grow.

Cream longhairs should have no stripes of any kind and no markings of another colour in their coat. Blue-cream longhairs are invariably females. Both colours should run into one another, and not be sharply defined. If cream-coloured animals are mated with one another, there is the danger that within a few generations stripes will begin to appear. A cream-coloured queen should preferably be mated with a pale blue tom.

The leading types of Red self and Red tabby longhairs are produced in England. They have suffered a marked decline in the rest of Europe. Beware of crossing them with cream-coloured partners. The results will be acceptable for registration only in the Experimental Standard. Recommended crossings are Red self with Red tabby, Red self and Red tabby with Black or Tortoiseshell, Black with Tortoiseshell. Crossings of Chinchilla with Blue will not be recognised as Chinchilla, but can be registered under Standard No. 13a in the Experimental Register.

New breeds and colourings have in the past occurred more or less by accident, as the result of a chance mutation or an unintended mating. Nowadays, there is an increasing tendency to plan breeding on the basis of genetic computation. Pedigrees must conform to a certain standard, that is to an ideal type established by breeders. The problem of where the borderline between a house cat and a pedigree cat lies can only be determined by saying that a house cat, which corresponds to the standard of a British Shorthair and fulfils several other requirements of the pedigree cat breeders' clubs, can also be a pedigree cat.

The registration bodies and the various breed and regional cat clubs which have grown up in every country lay down strict regulations for the conduct of shows, the awarding of prizes and the establishment of breeds. The very first cat show was held in London in 1871 and Britain still tends to lead in Cat Fancy affairs but there are considerable differences in what is allowed by the various organisations.

Some authorities allow the cat's pen at a show to be decked out to set the cat to best advantage and to have such toys and other ornaments as the breeder wishes to put in with the cat, but in Britain a white blanket, a white ribbon to attach an identification tag around the cat's neck, litter tray and food and water bowls are all that is permitted. All cats must start with the same conditions. A piece of plastic may be placed across the front of the pen if owners want to stop visitors from trying to touch their cats and this may also help to restrict the transference of infection.

Naturally a cat must be healthy to compete in a show if it is to stand any chance of success but when so many animals are gathered together no risks can be taken and at British shows all cats are inspected by a veterinary surgeon before they are allowed in. Sadly, nervousness or the rigours of the journey may sometimes make a cat behave as though it has the symptoms of an illness and cause the veterinary surgeon to debar it but that is better than risking spreading a disease.

You can find announcements of shows in the British paper *Fur and Feather* and in American journals such as *Cats Magazine* as well as in your local newspaper. Only registered cats can be entered and you will have to write in for entrance forms and may have to pay an entrance fee. Classes may vary from show to show and cater for experts and for novices.

The beauty of the cat should surely be the only consideration in all breeding activity. So many colour variations already exist that it is difficult even for the specialist to keep track of them all. A genuine new breed is extremely rare. Existing breeds and types must be improved and kept at their peak. Furthermore the pairing of two international champions will by no means necessarily guarantee a champion offspring. The animals to be crossed should not necessarily always be prize specimens, but should be of robust health and have particular characteristics and distinguishing features, in order to improve or maintain an existing breed.

The view commonly held among dog-breeders, in particular, that if a pedigree mates with a mongrel subsequent litters will somehow be affected or influenced and consequently make the pedigree bitch useless for breeding, has no scientific foundation whatsoever. Telegony, as this is called, in all animals, pedigree cats included, is mere superstition.

A mating should always be carefully planned. Choose a tom whose characteristics will complement those of your queen and correct any faults that she may have. Discuss the arrangements with the stud owner well before you expect your cat to come on heat so that when the time arrives you will be able to organise things quickly. Of course, if just at that time the tom is with another queen you may be unlucky and have to choose another stud or wait until the queen comes on heat again, but it is surprising how seldom this seems to happen.

You will have to pay a stud fee and for the boarding of the cat but, if your cat does not conceive, many stud owners will permit a second visit without a further stud fee. You must obtain a copy of the stud tom's pedigree so that you can list the parentage on both sides when you register any subsequent births.

There is nothing to stop you calling your cat whatever you like but for its registered name you will have to choose one that is not already in use. The usual practice is to submit several alternatives in case your favourite is not allowed. Naturally the more common the name the more chance there is of it being denied. Many breeders register a name for their cattery, known as a 'prefix' which cannot be used by any other breeder and this enables them to be sure that they have no naming problems in registration. It also enables anyone to recognise the line from which that cat comes when they see the prefix in the pedigree.

The follies of fashion   In a publication addressed to animal lovers, this subject should not really arise. Decadence in a variety of forms, is, however, on the increase, arising from unhealthy, exaggerated affection for an animal, so that the subject does deserve mention here.

In the USA alone, there are about 700 million house pets today, that is three times the human population of the country. This includes 40 million cats and the same number of dogs, 15 million birds, 600 million fish and some 10 million other pets. In the Federal Republic of Germany the numbers are approximately 4 million dogs, 3 million cats, 10 million birds and other animals besides. All these house pets have $ 4,000 million spent on them annually in the USA, £ 200 million in England, £ 150 million in the Federal Republic of Germany, and £ 60 million in France. These sums are large enough to affect a country's economic balance sheet. In the USA $ 1,600 million a year are spent at present on commercially prepared dog and cat foods alone. So far, so good.

The negative side emerges, however, when one considers that more and more people nowadays keep a pet merely as a status symbol. This is borne out not only by figures disclosing that, again in the USA, there is an annual turnover of £ 26 million on 'clothing' for example, and the same amount for 'jewellery' for house pets.

There is nothing wrong with the idea of animal cemeteries. In America there are currently more than 400 of these, with a new one being opened every two months. Is it really necessary, however, to have 'burial institutions' earning some £ 200 from the de-luxe burial, for example, of a dog or a cat? In Farmingdale, USA, such an institution operates under the slogan of, 'We deliver absolutely everything you expect from a human burial, bar the church ceremony!' An English magazine published a photo, showing two cats seated side by side on a table, covered with a white cloth, with two candlesticks on it containing burning candles. A man with a Bible, and another man playing the piano in the background completed the scene. The 'appropriate' text being read from the Bible was about the creation of the animals. The caption read: 'Cats' wedding!' The insertion was published on behalf of an association promoting 'Rights for Cats'. After the wedding, the cat owner announced: 'I am sure that Mimi will soon be having kittens from Blackie, and in my opinion, it is so much more proper, if they're married.'

Cute cat clothes, collars in alluring colours, hats and similar decadent nonsense appear on the market. Sickening humanised products for the dog market range from 11 different shades of nail varnish for manicured dogs' claws, to various perfumes, hair dyes in the most sophisticated tones, and special dog mouthwashes.

In Japan there is a flourishing animal hospital for dogs and cats. The hospital contains 50 rooms, including four luxury suites with soft beds, colour television, bath, lamps, paintings, silk quilts and fresh flowers daily—for 'only' £ 7.50 a day. In Los Angeles, a Persian tom which broke a tooth by crashing through a window, was fitted with a gold tooth for $200. Incidents such as these may cause a smile—but are they really a laughing matter?

80 A White longhair tom with copper-coloured eyes. Varieties with blue eyes and with one eye of each colour are also recognised.

81　This young White long-hair is already showing the massive, stocky look required in pedigree long-haired cats.

82　A Black longhair's lustrous coat must show no tinge of rustiness or specks of lighter fur if it is to meet show standards.

84 The round, broad head, short nose and small but wide-set ears of this cat are all characteristic of the long-hair type.

85 Long-haired cats should have sturdy bodies but this Red longhair tom's full coat makes him look even more massive.

88 *This Red longhair kitten has not yet developed its full, silky coat.*

89 *This Cream longhair has a delicately shaded coat and its exceptionally long whiskers give it an additional appeal.*

84 The round, broad head, short nose and small but wide-set ears of this cat are all characteristic of the long-hair type.

85 Long-haired cats should have sturdy bodies but this Red longhair tom's full coat makes him look even more massive.

86 Cream longhair
87 Silver tabby longhair

88   *This Red longhair kitten has not yet developed its full, silky coat.*

89   *This Cream longhair has a delicately shaded coat and its exceptionally long whiskers give it an additional appeal.*

90   *The Red tabby was once thought to be a male-only breed but this has been proved untrue.*

91 Red tabby longhair

92 Tortoiseshell and white longhair

Overleaf:
93 The Brown tabby longhair should have a coat of a rich tawny brown marked with black.

94 The Smoke should have an unmarked black face and feet with a ruff, ear tufts of silver and the body shading to silver on the sides.

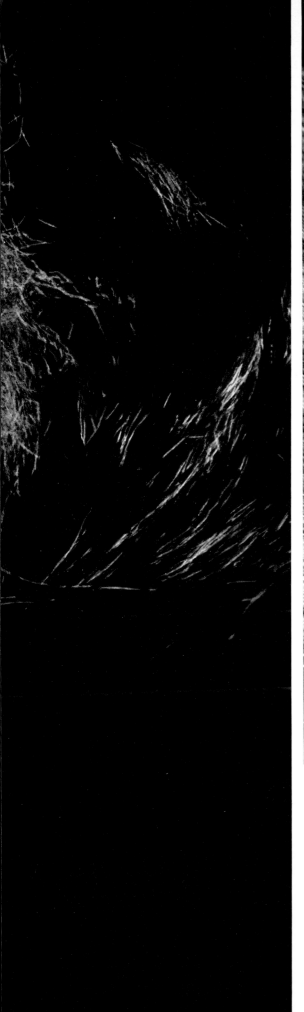

95/96 *Brown tabby longhair: there are many attractive tabby cats but those with markings which conform to the breed standards are far less common.*

97   This Silver tabby longhair is beginning to lose its patience. Show standards require the Silver tabby's eyes to be green or hazel in colour.

98   The pure white undercoat of the Chinchilla is overlaid by a black-tipped coat giving this delicate effect. The eyes should be emerald or blue-green in colour.

99 *Tortoiseshell longhair*

100 When the black, red and cream coat of the tortoiseshell is mixed with white the cat is known as a Tortoiseshell and white. This cat's colouring would not qualify it for the breed standard—proof that it is not only pedigree cats that are attractive.

101   *A Blue-cream longhair*

102   *The Shell cameo, a longhair from the United States which has not yet been recognised in Britain, has a white undercoat overlaid with a coat lightly tipped with red.*

103/104 Cat shows are becoming very popular drawing more and more entries and spectators. Rules vary from country to country and association to association. Sometimes pens may be decorated, often they are carefully separated from each other to reduce the risk of infection, but whether in Germany, as here, or elsewhere, the judges will look for high standards in appearance, condition and temperament.

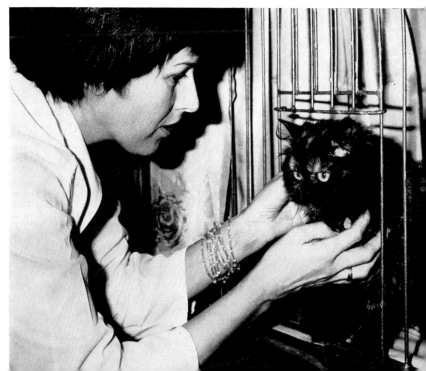

113   *Shell cameo longhair*

114   *Tortoiseshell and white longhair*

103/104 Cat shows are becoming
very popular drawing more and more
entries and spectators. Rules vary from
country to country and association to
association. Sometimes pens may be
decorated, often they are carefully
separated from each other to reduce the
risk of infection, but whether in
Germany, as here, or elsewhere, the
judges will look for high standards in
appearance, condition and temperament.

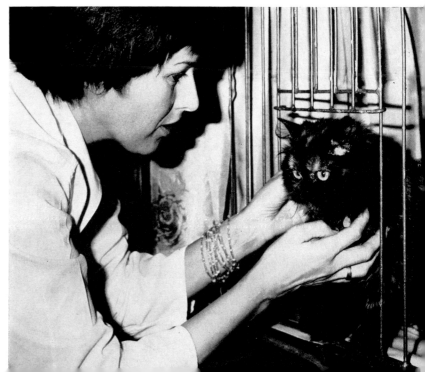

109/110   A Tabby point Siamese. Not yet recognised by all the American societies, this is now becoming a popular breed in Britain and Europe, its elegant looks and attractive markings giving it a strong appeal. This young cat's markings will strengthen and darken a little as it gets older.

103/104 Cat shows are becoming
very popular drawing more and more
entries and spectators. Rules vary from
country to country and association to
association. Sometimes pens may be
decorated, often they are carefully
separated from each other to reduce the
risk of infection, but whether in
Germany, as here, or elsewhere, the
judges will look for high standards in
appearance, condition and temperament.

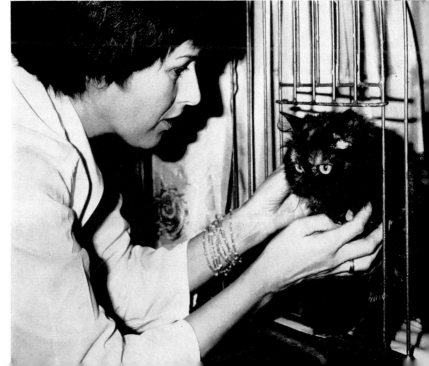

105/106/107/108 *Cats love to climb inside things, whether basket, cardboard box or roll of fabric. Sometimes it is to find a quiet place to be alone but often it is not so much to hide as to be sought and they are soon calling 'come and find me' to their playmates or their owner.*

109/110   A Tabby point Siamese.
Not yet recognised by all the American
societies, this is now becoming a popular
breed in Britain and Europe, its elegant
looks and attractive markings giving it
a strong appeal. This young cat's
markings will strengthen and darken
a little as it gets older.

111   Show cats must be patient and even-tempered to tolerate the travelling, the long hours in the exhibition hall, being handled by unknown judges and stared at by hundreds of other strangers.

112   White longhairs need particular care if they are to be shown, for their fur easily stains.

115/116 *A Silver tabby longhair.*
Silver tabbies have gained a reputation
with some breeders for being particularly
good-tempered. Kittens born with partic-
ularly clear markings do not usually
mature into well-marked cats in this
particular breed.

117 *A Bi-coloured shorthair. Although black and white bi-colours are probably the type most widely seen the standard allows for any solid colour and white.*

118 *A Tortoiseshell longhair*

Overleaf:

119 *A Tabby longhair*

120 *A Tortoiseshell longhair*

121   *Show days are bad enough but*
all this photography is really intolerable!

122   *A Smoke longhair*

126 *This Tabby short-hair has white in his coat, which is not officially permitted in Brown tabbies, but that does not stop him from being a lively and attractive cat.*

123 *A Red tabby shorthair tom (left)*
and a Brown tabby shorthair (right)

124 *A Cream longhair*

125 *A Tortoiseshell and white longhair*

126 This Tabby short-hair has white in his coat, which is not officially permitted in Brown tabbies, but that does not stop him from being a lively and attractive cat.

Graham R. Tomson ## The Fireside Sphinx

Half loving-kindliness and half disdain,
Thou comest to my call serenely suave,
With humming speech and gracious gestures grace,
In salutation courtly and urbane:

Yet must I humble me thy grace to gain—
For wiles may win thee, but no arts enslave,
And nowhere gladly thou abidest save
Where naught disturbs the concord of thy reign.

Sphinx of my quiet hearth! who deignst to dwell
Friend of my toil, companion of mine ease,
Thine is the lore of Ra and Rameses;
That men forget dost thou remember well,
Beholden still in blinking reveries,
With sombre sea-green gaze inscrutable.

Cat care

Sleep and sleeping quarters

Study of the rhythm of the daytime activity both of the wild cat and of the domesticated house cat has shown that cats belong to the group of animals that is lively in the daytime, but more particularly at dusk. By the term rhythm of activities, we mean the regular alternation in behaviour of an animal with a day-night cycle. These activities are influenced by numerous factors such as constitution, age, sex, environmental factors and time of year, or the physiological condition of the individual, such as hunger, fatigue, excitement, reproductive urge and the like. A further, very influential factor is that the pet easily and very rapidly adapts itself to the habits of the human beings around it and their daily rhythm. In normal circumstances the most active time for the cat is the afternoon and evening. Apart from when it is in season, the cat sleeps through the night. Admittedly, even in the daytime there are periods of varying length, when it rests or sleeps. Most of all, it loves to lie for hours basking undisturbed in the sun.

Many scientists see sleep as a form of activity, and not as a passive state in an animal. Consciousness and, to a certain extent, sensitivity to pain, are suspended in sleep, and the rate of breathing and the pulse rate are lowered. Certain active functions are, however, fulfilled during sleep which provides a restorative effect. Although general receptivity to external stimuli is considerably reduced, it does not by any means cease entirely. A 'filtering' of external stimuli takes place. Danger stimuli or, with mother cats, for example, noise or movements from newborn kittens, unusual sounds, light stimuli, and the like, will immediately rouse the cat from sleep. In animals it is very often difficult to tell the difference between a state of genuine sleep and mere resting.

Sleeping position The sleeping position of the house cat is flat on its side, with legs more or less outstretched, or, curled right up in a ball with the head placed on the tail beside the back legs. The sleeping cat will often cover its eyes with its paws. One resting position, which is sometimes also adopted in sleep is lying flat with the paws either outstretched or doubled under, and the tail curled round facing towards the front.

At this point, just a word on the subject of dreams and animals in general, since this topic has frequently been raised with regard to cats. Cats are often seen to move their

157

paws, tails, ears and are even heard to make noises in their sleep. Does this suggest they have dreams comparable to human dreams? Research into human dreams is complex enough in itself, inferences as to animals are even more so and pose a virtually insoluble problem. There are two factors which play an important role in human dreams—the recollection of actual experiences and the imagination or fantasy that creates new dream images. To a limited extent, a cat also possesses a memory. Fantasy, however, requires the faculty of abstract thought and imagination, the existence of which it has not so far been possible to prove in an animal. Encephalograms have shown that while a person dreams all his muscles are relaxed and that he is lying completely undisturbed. Muscular movements occur only in the phase of light sleep, when no dreams occur. The movements are not, therefore, the expression of a dream, but reactions to internal stimuli, which are not accompanied by emotions. A definitive answer to the question of whether or not animals dream cannot as yet be given.

Waking Cats yawn frequently and hugely, both before falling asleep and again on waking. As they do so, they usually lick their lips and chest briefly. If the cat has raised itself from its sleeping position, it will stretch itself with its back fully arched, and legs close together. But it also indulges in stretching, with its hindquarters in the air and its forepaws extended. This procedure is often followed by the reverse action, with the forequarters erect, and the back paws stretched back flat, and even while it is taking its first steps, first one back leg and then the other will still be fully stretched out backwards. This may then be followed by sharpening of the claws, shaking of the legs or shaking the whole body. The cat likes stretching up against some object or the legs of its owner, and may attempt to exercise its claws as it does so.

If we want to pick the cat up, we should never do so by the front paws alone. A cat has no collar-bone, and consequently its front extremities are not as firmly anchored as our arms. Picking it up in the wrong way can very easily dislocate its legs. Although it is quite acceptable for kittens to be picked up by the scruff of the neck, this is not advisable for fully-grown animals. Either pick the cat up by the back of the neck with one hand, and place the other hand on the fur of its lumbar region, encircling its hindquarters, or place one hand under the chest, supporting the hindquarters with the other hand.

Sleeping quarters The most suitable sleeping quarters for the cat are a place in the house that is sheltered from cold and, in particular, from draughts. Here place a small wooden box, an old armchair or, better still, a wicker cat basket. Cats seem to like baskets very much, although fibreglass containers are more hygienic! If the basket is then lined with a blanket, a pillow or old clothes, it will quickly be accepted as a soft bed. It is important to keep the soft padding under constant scrutiny to prevent a stray flea that may have been brought in, from settling in it and breeding. Frequent washing and boiling is essential. The cat loves to have a fixed, regular spot of its own. Therefore its bed or resting place should be shifted only if absolutely necessary. The cat will find a favourite spot, where it can spend hours on end snoozing during the day. It will usually select an undisturbed, raised position, from where it can always observe everything.

There are two procedures that should never be adopted—a house cat should never be locked in the cellar at night, nor should it be left out of doors; however, it is equally unacceptable to take the cat into one's bed.

Looking after itself House cats, like all forms of wild cat, are scrupulous about personal hygiene. The soft, loose fur of the cat enables the supple musculature to function to the full. If it were covered by a firm, hard skin, the musculature could not develop in the same way. It is the perfect combination of very loose bone structure, supple musculature, and soft fur that gives the cat the requisite litheness and manoeuvrability. The very softness of the cat's fur unfortunately makes it commercially attractive, even though it is less durable than other pelts.

Function of the fur Although this fine fluffy fur is hardly water repellent (which is why the cat dislikes wetness and damp), it plays a very important role in conjunction with the skin in regulating the body temperature. The warm undercoat grows thicker in winter, whereas the guard hairs are less thick and resistant. In summer the under-fur becomes thinner and shorter, and all the warmth of the sun can be fully soaked up. The circulation of the blood through the skin also changes with the outdoor temperature. In winter a layer of insulating fat is deposited in the subcutaneous tissue to avoid heat loss.

The smoothness of the cat's fur prevents it from causing any sound as it slinks along in the undergrowth, stalking some prey. Mosquitoes, and flies, and similar nuisances do not

bother the cat, as it sits motionless in one spot. One function of the fur of both house and wild cats that should not be underestimated is to provide visual signals as part of its special body language. Any member of the species, and indeed many other animals, especially if they are enemies or prey, are able to interpret these 'signals'. The characteristic fluffing up of the hairs on the back and tail is an unmistakable indication of threatening and aggressive behaviour.

Grooming   The sensitive fur is constantly groomed by the cat with a series of instinctive actions. Paul Leyhausen has also made a detailed study of these grooming actions, comparing those of widely differing cat species. The simplest form of grooming he describes is nose licking. This consists of the tongue moving straight upwards and immediately withdrawing again. The nostrils are cleaned in this way, but this licking also removes disturbing nasal irritants. Washing the lips after eating and drinking is done by the tongue moving along the upper lip in a sideways action followed by a downwards movement into the corners of the mouth. Sneezing and wiping the nose with a paw remove stronger irritant smells and more extensive dirt.

The commonest form of grooming is licking the fur. Undisturbed, the cat will proceed in a precise and methodical manner. The rough tongue goes over the fur in long, powerful strokes, not only cleaning and smoothing, but moistening with saliva and drying again. The cat's supple body enables its tongue to reach almost everywhere. Only the head has to be washed by use of the moistened paw. This head washing follows a particularly unvarying 'ritual'. Although it may be interrupted at will, it will always be resumed in the same way. In a sitting position, the cat will lick and moisten the 'elbow side' of one of its forepaws, raised to an almost horizontal position. This is followed by wiping the paw in a circular motion sideways across the nose. It then repeats the moistening and resumes somewhat higher up the face. It continues, progressing upwards all the time. Only on the third occasion, at the earliest, does the paw go behind the ear and down across the forehead and eyes. No other form of body grooming has such an unwaveringly precise sequence. Every other part of the body may be washed either individually or sometimes in between other actions. As a rule, however, 'washing' begins in the front and proceeds in a backwards direction. The eagerness with which the cat applies itself to this procedure, and the fact that it does not find it in any way irksome, can be

160

seen from the way in which it may very well transfer its grooming actions, and the licking in particular, to a human who happens to be close by.

The unbroken order of a typical sequence of grooming actions is described by Prof. Leyhausen as follows: licking of the shoulders and flanks, lower neck and breast, the arms from the elbows down towards the paws, then first the upper side of the forepaws and then the pads and the inward curling toes. Then, it nibbles between the widely splayed toes of the forepaws. This is followed by intensive head washing, the stomach is then rather fleetingly attended to, followed by a more thorough treatment of the anal region. The cat then washes its hindlegs, licking the insides, nibbling between the toes, and licking the outsides. Next comes the tail, which is licked and nibbled. As they nibble, the side teeth seize the fur and comb through it vigorously in the direction that the hair grows. After this the fur that has been combed is licked smooth again. In between all the licking there is intermittent scratching, especially on the chin, throat, cheeks, ears and sides of the neck.

A 'complete wash' such as this is usually performed before or after a rest period. Front paws, breast and face are thoroughly cleaned after a meal, and the anal region after using the dirt tray, after pairing and before, during and after giving birth.

Social grooming Cats that are kept together in the same home will indulge in social grooming, too, that is, they will groom each other. Mothers wash their young fairly vigorously, but the kittens, too, will lick each other and even their mother. And, as mentioned above, this kind of social grooming will even be extended to humans. If the cat is on one's lap while it is washing itself, the licking will carry on from its fur to one's own skin without a break.

In the process of this intensive washing with the rough tongue, a lot of hair is swallowed, especially during the period of seasonal moult. If these hairs form hairballs in the stomach this can be very dangerous for the cat. Giving the cat grass to eat in good time can make it vomit and thus rid the stomach of the troublesome hairs.

Licking the fur can, however, also be a transitional activity if the cat is intent on some quite different action, and is for some reason prevented or inhibited from carrying it out. For example, an unexpected light smack may unleash great indignation, which does not express itself in flight or attack, but results in vigorous washing. Body grooming is almost always carried out in a sitting position; licking the flanks, stomach and legs, tail and forelegs is frequently done in a prone position. Standing cats usually wash sketchily, mostly as a 'transitional' activity.

Even kittens that have been reared in total isolation from the mother know, without any experience, how to perform the body grooming, in exactly the same way that an adult cat does. This proves that it must be an inborn action. This is not to say that all the separate actions involved are mastered together by a particular time, rather they are acquired in succession, in relation to the stage of development that the kitten has reached.

The first, and simplest, action of scratching behind the ear with the hind paw can already be observed, albeit in a somewhat clumsy form, by about the 12th day, even before any attempt has been made at coordinated walking, which usually begins on about the 16th day. Mostly the kitten simply tips over as it tries to bring the back paw behind its ear. It takes until it is 28–30 days old to perfect this action. Face washing is not attempted until the 26th day and will also be perfect between the 28th and 30th day. The development and mastery of these individual actions can, in fact, be pin-pointed almost to the day.

Coat and skin undergo a process of constant renewal. Maximum care and a carefully balanced diet are a positive aid to this process. Persistent overfeeding can cause the skin to stretch, resulting in a loss of elasticity. Excessive deposits of fat in the subcutaneous tissue inhibit the essential control of body temperature which can ultimately result in damage to the coat. This in turn will encourage bacterial infections and fungus diseases. Constant overfeeding inhibits the renewal process of skin and coat, resulting in dry skin, dandruff and brittle fur, often with a loss of colour, and the skin is also inclined to bleed easily. The cat scratches increasingly, and it is almost impossible to prevent infection.

Deficiency of certain vitamins often has a severe effect on skin and hair. If, for example, there is a deficiency of B_2—riboflavin—the epidermis containing the hair follicles atrophies, affecting the sebaceous glands. The hair becomes uneven, unkempt and dull as a result. In the absence of Vitamin B Complex lack of nicotinic acid can produce excessive skin growth, so-called hyperkeratosis, and hair-loss; and lack of pantothenic acid causes the hair to fall out, especially around the eyes, the coat becoming hard and lustreless, with a marked loss of colour. Vitamin A deficiency, usually coupled with B deficiency, likewise leads to hyperkeratosis and the formation of bald and scaly patches in the coat. The undercoat falls out more than the guard hairs. However, excessive doses of Vitamin A are equally harmful and can, for example, bring the normal keratin formation to a complete standstill. Mineral zinc deficiency results in inflammation of the skin and hairloss. In kittens, in particular, this causes thin hair and reddened skin. Copper deficiency results in loss of pigmentation with discolouration of skin and hair. Insufficient manganese makes the coat hairs grey; too much, however, makes a light coat turn dark as a result of excessive pigmentation. Any kind of skin disease affects the coat. Thus a severe inflammation of the skin can destroy pigment cells, so that the coat turns completely white; mild inflammation on the other hand, stimulates the production of pigmentation, producing a darker coat. The latter frequently appears after wounds or surgical operations on Siamese. This type of increased pigment production may stop after the first or second moult.

Simple, but indispensable forms of grooming are combing and brushing, especially with long-haired cats. On their own it is difficult for these cats to keep their beautiful, fine long hair in good condition. Daily combing and brushing is essential during the period of seasonal moult. This considerably accelerates the moulting process and prevents the cat swallowing excessive amounts of dead hair. In addition, it massages the skin, which improves the circulation, providing favourable conditions for the growth of new hair.

Combing The spring moult often starts as early as January, with the denser undercoat loosening and dropping out. Using a steel comb, comb the coat layer by layer right **162**

through to the skin. Every four to six weeks a little talc powder may be applied between the layers. The talc is then combed out again, making the coat softer and fluffy. The most difficult areas such as the stomach, the groin area and the armpits should be combed first, since the cat will only voluntarily submit to the procedure for a short while; back, neck and breast can be done at the end, since this is easier and does not require the co-operation of the cat. Combing every other day, and sometimes even twice a week is adequate. Once the hair almost ceases to come out, the combing may be done less frequently. If matted areas should form on the belly, groin or in the armpits, these should be removed very carefully with a pair of fine scissors, to avoid hurting the skin. Knots are very difficult to remove. In any case, it is important to make absolutely sure that the cause is in fact only matting or knots. In its summer coat, a long-haired cat that is well cared for and frequently combed may even resemble a shorthair. However, in winter it has a longer, healthy coat. Even a short-haired cat should have the old, dead hairs removed while it is moulting, and a brush is all that is needed for this purpose.

Moulting As the outer hairs die off at the beginning of autumn, a second seasonal moult begins. With longhairs, one should try to remove the dead hairs gently by hand. This can be done by moving the outstretched index finger and thumb up the coat, against the direction of the hairs. The tail should not be overlooked. At this time, Blue, Black and Silver tabbys develop a definite rusty tinge. Even the ticking of Chinchillas looks rust-coloured. Creams show red spots in their hair.

If intending to exhibit a Black, Tortoiseshell, Red self, Striped or Brown tabby in a show, it should be powdered a few days before the show and the hair thoroughly brushed out. Most cats really enjoy brushing. The best brushes for this purpose are either rubber or natural bristle. If there is the slightest suspicion of fleas, a fine-tooth comb should be used. If the suspicion is confirmed, and this can occur even with the best-kept pedigree cat, then the measures suggested in the section on skin parasites in the chapter on cat-ailments should be adopted.

163

Some cat owners use a small vacuum cleaner for grooming the coat. Once the cat has got used to the noise, it will willingly submit to this. Dirt, dust, loose hairs and vermin are all removed painlessly, surely and quickly by this means.

With all these forms of beauty grooming, one should never forget that it is the owner, not the cat, who is concerned with the beauty of the animal's appearance.

Ears   The cat has exceptionally acute hearing. Its extremely mobile outer ears are receptive to sound waves coming from a considerable distance. This is why cats are so sensitive to loud noises or voices. They can assess the distance and the direction from which a noise has come with great accuracy, which is extremely useful when they are stalking prey.

Although tufts of hair protect the outer ear from penetration by foreign bodies, cats' ears need special care and attention. Infestation by irritating and harmful mites as well as the build-up of wax causing inflammation and blockages all too commonly occur. If the cat seems frequently to be scratching vigorously at its ear, often shaking its head as well, then some kind of ear trouble is indicated. A preventive measure is to dab carefully all round the outer ear with a cotton wool bud, (or a match wrapped in cotton wool) soaked in skin oil. Inflammation of the ear can usually be avoided by keeping the cat well away from draughts.

Eyes and nose   A second excellent sensory organ is the eye. The cat has very good vision. There are 400,000 vision elements or cells per square millimetre in the cat's eye. Behind the retina is an iridescent layer of pigment that increases the reflection of light. This also causes the cat's eyes to shine in the dark, if illuminated by any source of light. It has been proved that cats are able to distinguish colours—not all animals are able to do this. The pupil of the eye closes in the form of a vertical slit. The speed with which the size of the pupil changes from being round and wide open to the narrowest slit sufficiently protects the eye's sensitivity to light. In complete darkness, the cat can, however, not see any-thing—a minimum of light is necessary. The lively and constantly changing eyes of the cat, positioned in the front of the head, are what makes its face so expressive.

Normally the cat's eyes do not require any special care. If a speck of dirt has lodged in the corner of the eye, take a piece of clean cloth and wipe it away. If the cat has a cold, or is shedding its milk teeth, then there may often be a slight discharge of pus from the corner of the eye. Bathing with water is helpful in such cases. At one time boracic acid solution was recommended for this problem, but this should not be used (it is no longer used for humans either). Inflammation of the eye should, however, be given very careful consideration, for it may easily be caused by some more serious illness.

The cat has a fairly well developed sense of smell, the main function of which is sexual. When they are in season, tom cats and queens find each other by their very powerful sexual odour. Naturally, the cat is also able to detect the odours of other animals, and of humans. Certain smells even have an intoxicating effect on the cat. The aroma of valerian, for example, or of catmint is known to produce this effect in many cats. But human perspiration appears to have a similar effect. Sometimes the cat will make a determined attempt to crawl into the hollow of a sweaty human armpit.

127 *Kittens usually sleep curled up against their mother for warmth or snuggled against each other. The kitten does not seem to have been so quick in waking up as its mother.*

127 *Kittens usually sleep curled up against their mother for warmth or snuggled against each other. The kitten does not seem to have been so quick in waking up as its mother.*

128 Tired animals yawn just like humans and cats will often stretch thoroughly when they wake.

129 A mother cat cleans up her kittens at every opportunity.

130 The kittens develop the various instinctive grooming procedures in a particular order.

131/132/133/134 Having found a safe and secure place to settle down and wash, the paw is usually moistened first and used to give the face a thorough scrubbing. The eyes are often kept closed through much of the procedure.

135/136 *A cat does not like being disturbed while grooming itself. If it breaks off to check on a sound or interruption it will often maintain its position and, if all is clear, return immediately to its toilet.*

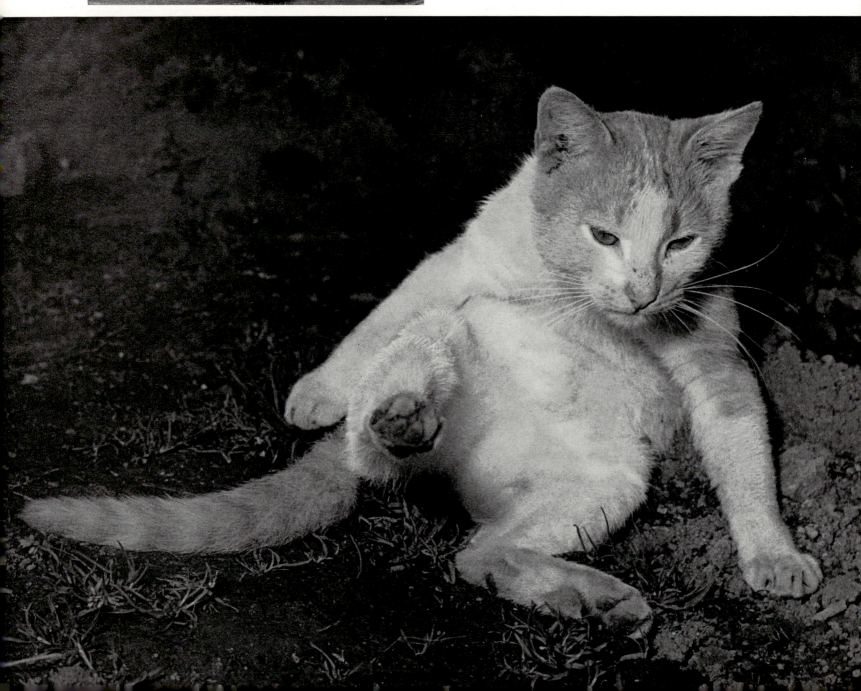

137/138 *The cat's agility enables it to reach every part of its body either with its tongue or by scrubbing with its moistened paws, cleaning its fur and smoothing it as if with a brush. After a long grooming session a cat will frequently take a nap.*

139/140/141/142 *Their good balance and sharp claws make cats efficient climbers. If cats and kittens have plenty of opportunity to climb trees they will not need to have their claws trimmed.*

143/144 Cats will often ignore a stationary object but moving things that are smaller than themselves can instantly provoke a game, rousing the instincts of the natural predator to chase and catch.

145 This long-haired coat demonstrates the need for daily grooming if it is to look light and fluffy and remain unmatted. The brushing also stimulates the circulation and helps keep skin healthy.

The cat's whiskers are used to test and examine objects with the utmost care. The coarse wiry hairs on the upper and lower lip, on the eyebrows and paws are organs of touch which help the cat to find its way silently and in complete darkness, without bumping into anything. The nose and the whiskers do not require any special care.

Teeth Cats' teeth are frequently neglected. Many cat lovers are not even aware that cats shed their milk teeth. This change to permanent dentition is quite often linked with changes in the kittens' behaviour. During this period they become more prone to illness. They may even revert to soiling. Regular inspection of the mouth will reveal decay in good time. Dental infections or fistulae, should be treated by a veterinary surgeon. If the milk teeth are not shed and obstinately remain beside the permanent ones, simply rocking them is often enough to make them come out. Tartar frequently forms on the teeth of adult cats. In the initial stages, a nail file applied to the upper rim of the tooth and pressed firmly against it, may sometimes make the plaque separate off. Care must be taken in the advanced stages, however, since by then teeth may be loose, there may be inflammation of the gums and bleeding can very easily occur. In this case it is best to seek the advice of the veterinary surgeon.

Claws Care of the claws can normally be carried out by the cat itself. We can assist this care indirectly by providing the necessary objects, such as a scratching post. In the wild, the claws are sharpened on larger trees or boughs. With the forepaw splayed out wide, the claws are sunk into the rough wood and dragged forcefully backwards. In doing this, the cat sheds the worn parts of the claw, sharpens the smooth part, and also removes any dirt or food that adheres to the furrowed underside of the claw.

The cat's claw is constructed in such a way that the worn, upper shell, shoe-like, can be slipped off from the newly-grown layer underneath. If the worn shell is not shed regularly, it will continue to grow, and the curved tips of the claws may grow into the toes. If this happens, surgery by the veterinary surgeon will be necessary. On no account must the newly-grown lower claw be damaged in the process. Once the old shell has been removed, a perfectly developed new claw will be revealed underneath. Occasionally cats that get no exercise on hard surfaces may grow claws quicker than they wear them down and need them trimmed. This should be done with clippers and great care must be taken not to cut into the quick. A veterinary surgeon will show you how.

Newborn kittens have hollow, blunt sheaths over their tiny, pointed claws, which dry and drop off within the first 24 hours of life. Their function is to protect the maternal passages while the kitten is being born. These parchment-like, comma-shaped, little sheaths are frequently overlooked.

The cat likes sharpening its claws on carpets, curtains, upholstery, wicker chairs and wooden stools. Right from the start it is important to make the cat perform this necessary action where we want it to. The easiest thing to do is to make over a worn-out piece of furniture to the cat specifically for this purpose, but a scratching post is better. A simple log with its rough bark intact, well secured at a slight angle on a firm base is the ideal solution. But a similar piece of apparatus is easy enough to make. Sometimes a tough, old board, rough and firm, but not too hard or brittle, will suffice. Such a board can also be covered with several old socks or old cloths, or an old sisal runner can be wrapped

round it and nailed fast at the back, and this can be set up securely on a base. Towelling or the like should not be used, since the cat can catch its claws in it and get caught up. Cutting the claws is not normally necessary, and is not recommended. If the cat is allowed out in winter, one should watch out that the steps, stairs and roads where it is likely to go are not strewn with thawing salt, as this is very harmful to the cat's paws. On the other hand, in the summer flowerbeds treated with manure or weed-killer and pesticides constitute a danger. The dust from these settles on the cat's fur as it passes, and, subsequently, when it washes itself, it will swallow these dangerous substances.

Tail The cat's tail is the most important indicator of its mood, reflecting the slightest excitation. It is the cat's most significant means of expressing itself. Well-being, affection, dislike, pain, aggressiveness or threat, excited watchfulness or the intention to run away, all this can be 'read' from the tail of a cat. It is used to assist balance when the cat is climbing, and is an important steering organ in running, springing or leaping down. Most cats will not allow their tails to be touched. Apart from combing and brushing the tail hairs, long-haired cats and pedigrees in particular should have their tails and especially the underside powdered once a week in order to remove the secretion of the sex organs which otherwise gums up the fur as it discharges.

Cats do not like water, apart from a few exceptions, but can swim in an emergency. As a rule, the ordinary house cat will avoid even the smallest puddle, and should the tiniest drop of water fall on its paw, it will shake it repeatedly.

Baths— does the cat need them?

The cat detests dew-soaked grass, and something must really be wrong to induce it to tear through it at full tilt. The term 'cat's lick', used when referring to a person who tends to wash as quickly and lightly as possible, derives from the cat's attitude to water. In fact cats will spend many hours cleaning and grooming themselves.

As a rule it is not necessary to bath a cat. However, if a bath should really be essential, for example if it has got completely covered in dirt, or in certain cases of skin disease when the veterinary surgeon insists on the cat being bathed, or when a long-haired cat is about to be exhibited in a show and a bath seems to be indicated, certain procedures should be followed to make the process more tolerable for the animal.

A rubber mat or bath mat should be placed along the bottom of the tub, to give the cat something to sink its claws into. The water temperature will depend to some extent on the time of year. At the height of summer, hand-hot water will be adequate, at other times it should be heated to about 35°C (95°F). The water level need be no more than hand high, and should in no case reach above the cat's neck. Washing agents should be free of alkali or tar preparations. Both perfumed and medicated soap should be avoided, since soap dissolves the natural oils in the cat's hairs, making the hair dry, which can lead to skin irritations. Baby soap or egg or oil shampoos are all suitable, but keep cats away from anything containing carbolic. When soaping the cat, care should be taken to avoid any getting in the cat's eyes. The soaping should be followed by thorough rinsing, until the water runs clear. The cat should be in a warm and draught-free room, but should not be left to dry itself. A hairdryer is ideal for drying the cat after a bath but the cat must be accustomed to it, otherwise it may take to its heels, and be permanently terrified of bathing. The hair must be dried right down as far as the skin. It should be continuously brushed and combed, while the dryer is being used. The skin should be massaged all the time to stimulate the circulation, and keep the cat warm. Even if the cat returns home rain-soaked, it should be towelled dry and given a thorough brushing.

In this way, despite their inherent dislike of water, cats can be kept in good health, either after a necessary bath or after being caught in a rain shower.

Ink and brush drawing by Joseph Hegenbarth

T. S. Eliot   # The Song of the Jellicles

Jellicle Cats come out to-night
Jellicle Cats come one come all:
The Jellicle Moon is shining bright—
Jellicles come to the Jellicle Ball.

Jellicle Cats are black and white,
Jellicle Cats are rather small;
Jellicle Cats are merry and bright,
And pleasant to hear when they caterwaul.
Jellicle Cats have cheerful faces,
Jellicle Cats have bright black eyes;
They like to practise their airs and graces
And wait for the Jellicle Moon to rise.

Jellicle Cats develop slowly,
Jellicle Cats are not too big;
Jellicle Cats are roly-poly,
They know how to dance a gavotte and a jig.
Until the Jellicle Moon appears
They make their toilette and take their repose:
Jellicles wash behind their ears,
Jellicles dry between their toes.

Jellicle Cats are white and black,
Jellicle Cats are of moderate size;
Jellicles jump like a jumping-jack,
Jellicle Cats have moonlit eyes.
They're quiet enough in the morning hours,
They're quiet enough in the afternoon,
Reserving their terpsichorean powers
To dance by the light of the Jellicle Moon.

Jellicle Cats are black and white,
Jellicle Cats (as I said) are small;
If it happens to be a stormy night
They will practise a caper or two in the hall.
If it happens the sun is shining bright
You would say they had nothing to do at all:
They are resting and saving themselves to be right
For the Jellicle Moon and the Jellicle Ball.

Sexual life and reproduction

Sexual behaviour in natural mating

When the cat is in season or on heat, both the tom, and in some cases the female cat too, will wander far afield. This unusual roving is caused by the onset of heat and the urgency that drives the two sexes together. In cats it is almost invariably the females that are the most active. Mature females in season will 'call' the toms over long distances with their loud, clear and characteristic 'yowling'. The female will at first fight off the tom by spitting, squalling and striking out with her claws. Once the two have drawn nearer to each other, both will make another typical, purring sound, sometimes mistaken for growling. Part of the courtship ritual, which stimulates the female, is a kind of coquettish flight, whereby she will retreat a little and then call the tom again. If the female has reached the stage in heat when she is prepared to mate, she will then invite him outright. Both extend their heads and rub them together. The female will gyrate from side to side, and finally present her raised hindquarters to the nose of the tom. The hindlegs will paw the ground excitedly. The tail is turned aside to reveal fully the female sex organs. The tom will then mount her and in the excitement of pairing will bite the scruff of her neck. The act is soon completed, and the spitting queen will then dart at the retreating tom with claws outstretched.

The unpleasant 'spraying' by the tom mentioned earlier is his way of giving reciprocal information at this time as to his sexual arousal. Females, too, will frequently spray when in season. Both sexes have large glands around their rear, and in addition toms have an anal sac. The secretions of the sweat and sebaceous glands are mixed with urine to mark the cat's territory, but are also used to attract the sexes to each other. If cats living in an apartment have sprayed pieces of furniture, they may be discouraged from further acts of this kind by various household agents. A clove of garlic or a squeezed lemon skin can be rubbed repeatedly into the areas concerned. The scent of roses, carnations or lily of the valley or of certain aerosols are also supposed to deter cats from spraying.

However, a cat in season cannot be cured of its condition by any kind of tranquilliser. Nature is all-powerful!

Unlike the domestic dog, the cat is not a herd animal but an individualist. For this reason its social behaviour is comparatively unremarkable, except during its reproductive season or when raising kittens. As described by Prof. Leyhausen, queens display the nest-building instinct common to most mammals. Its sleeping quarters, its 'own' corner of the room or cage, are its 'home' in the literal sense of the word. From here it sets out, along firmly established paths, to all sorts of places which are of importance to it. These places are where the cat eats, where the litter tray is kept, where it rests, where it maintains a look-out, where it will wash thoroughly and where it will sun itself. Longer routes lead to hunting, mating and fighting areas. Now it may well happen that these longer routes will intersect those of other cats. The traffic then becomes visual, that is, it is kept under observation. The cat will sit and watch until the other cat has disappeared, before setting out on the same path itself. If a sudden, unexpected meeting does take place, however, they may well come to blows. Females tend to be far readier than toms to fight with each other.

When two cats meet, it is easy to tell which of the two is the underlying. As a rule it is the cat that is straying on to alien territory. It does not look straight at the other cat, but looks around, as if completely unconcerned. Slowly, sometimes almost as if in slow motion, it will retreat from the dominant cat. Only a mother cat rearing a newborn litter will actually resort to physical defence of her 'home'.

By marking stones, trees, bushes and other objects with urine, cats inform each other about the use of ways and provide a means of avoiding sudden unexpected encounters. The hierarchy between cats is extremely complex and difficult to ascertain. There are differences of time and place, and the most diverse causes will establish a hierarchy that may often be quite flexible.

If a number of cats are at home in a certain area then a situation of permanent tension can be produced, leading to constant agitation in all concerned.

The cat's social behaviour

A confrontation between two tomcats (after H. Knappe)

Fighting between toms To intervene unaided in a fight between two toms is virtually impossible. Pouring a bucketful of cold water over them is the only certain way of separating the antagonists. Sometimes a blanket or coat thrown on top of them may also do the trick.

A soon as a growing tom reaches sexual maturity it will be challenged to fight by any old-established tom living in the same area. Once they have established which of the two is dominant, this superiority will always be acknowledged. If the challenge does lead to a fight the level of belligerence when the two meet will soon be reduced. The dominant animal will display its superiority, for example by sharpening its claws; at most there will be a small mock battle.

If two strange toms challenge each other, they will approach each other with arched backs and all four limbs fully outstretched, with ears pricked up and turned outwards and head raised. Their whole appearance is intended to be as intimidating as possible. The tail is turned downwards at right angles. The fixed gaze is directed at the opponent, the head moving slowly from side to side. As the tip of the tail lashes to and fro, they will draw nearer to each other. The noises they make are enough to make even human beings shudder. Long-drawn-out screams of varying intensity and pitch alternate with growling, shrieking and short battle cries. Suddenly, and quite unexpectedly, the two will hurl themselves at each other, sinking their claws blindly into the other's coat and biting at each other. The aim of each is to deal his opponent the dangerous bite in the neck. The weaker cat will usually turn on its back in order to improve its chances of defence. The fighting is also accompanied by loud screeches. In the majority of cases, the fight will break off just as suddenly as it began, giving the weaker of the opponents an opportunity to break away. Either it will remain sitting motionlessly, with ears flattened in a defensive position, or it will attempt to steal away slowly, almost in slow motion. If it does not do this, the two will fly at each other again. Two toms that are fighting are really out for blood; the intention is to injure the opponent. Such a confrontation is not merely a ritual exchange simply aimed at proving which is the dominant.

The familiar arched back supposedly denoting threat, is in fact merely an expression of indecision. The cat vacillates between moods of aggression and flight. Its forelegs are

183

withdrawn somewhat from its opponent and turned slightly to one side, while the hind-legs remain fixed on the same spot. This is accompanied by growling and spitting, flattened ears and baring of the teeth.

Owners of pedigree queens who intend to breed will be able to obtain a list of available stud toms from breed club secretaries. Naturally they will carefully match the tom to correct any faults or deficiences in their own cat.

Stud mating and breeding

Although some queens, especially orientals, come into season when they are very young, it is better to wait until they are 12–18 months old before allowing them to breed.

Queens should be given plenty of time to recuperate between litters and, although they may begin to call while still rearing their kittens, should not raise more than two litters a year. If a stud mating 'misses', a further mating with the same tom will usually be granted without a stud fee being charged—but this is not a right unless it is so agreed beforehand.

A queen remains in season for approximately four to ten days. The most favourable time for mating is between the sixth and eighth day. Since the mating of two partners hitherto unknown to each other may well be accompanied by biting and fighting, appropriate precautions must be taken in introducing the animals to each other. The safest arrangement is to have two adjacent compartments, so that the prospective partners can see and sniff each other, without having direct contact. Once the queen starts to roll at the fence separating her from the tom, the animals may be put together. The actual pairing will frequently follow very soon after, however, sometimes, despite the queen's apparent readiness, she may prove too intolerant. In this case the two must be left together for one to two days. One sign of the tom's readiness to mate is marking with urine, another is frequent licking of the erect penis.

If the queen has to be sent to a stud a long distance away, for example, in the case of an extremely rare breed, the journey must be very carefully planned. The date of the

184

visit should be fixed with the owner of the stud tom, having calculated the dates when the queen is expected to be in season. The queen should be accompanied if possible but if she has to be sent alone a very secure container should be used—a cat on heat will do her best to get out if she can. A label should indicate that the cat is to be collected, and not be forwarded via a carrier. The carrying basket should also have a label attached to it, saying 'Care—live animal', and another saying 'This side up', and in the case of a longer journey, requests or instructions for giving her a drink may be necessary.

Heat, pairing, pregnancy

The period when the female cat accepts the male (scientifically called oestrus, heat, or 'in season') normally occurs twice, or three times a year, mostly in February/March and in June, but in house cats can be much more frequent, especially among orientals which are not allowed to breed. The first receptive period may occur when the cat is only 6–9 months old. However, the cat is not physically mature, and hence not ready for breeding, until 12–15 months. A young tom is sexually mature at the age of 8–12 months. The heat period lasts between 4 and 10 days. It is only during this period that the animal's ovaries, controlled by hormones, are fully functional and produce egg cells that can be fertilised. Experienced toms are ready to mate all the year round, but frequently they too are affected by a cyclical process just as the queen is. One heat period can be immediately followed by another, but normally even a non-suckling queen will have an interval of several weeks or even months between two heat periods. After pregnancy, the queen will normally not come into season again for another two to five months. With cats that are kept isolated and shut away in flats, the heat periods may be more frequent.

During the heat period the cat will miaow constantly, rub itself against the legs of human beings or furniture, and will display the familiar kneading of the hindlegs, with the hindlegs bent under and the tail erect, and finally will roll over on to its back more and more frequently, and writhe about on the ground. Even the strongest tranquilliser will not alleviate the condition of the cat in season. The mounting of the receptive queen

185

by the tom proceeds in the manner described earlier, and usually there will be repeated pairings in order to ensure that copulation and subsequent conception really do take place. The cat on heat may also adopt its copulation posture if the owner strokes its back or presses its neck or back gently. The length of the gestation period, or pregnancy, can vary considerably from one cat to another. However there is no difference between short-haired and long-haired cats. In a survey of pregnancies the shortest gestation period observed was 54 days, the longest 74 days; 62 per cent of all cats observed carried for 62, 63 and 65 days; 24 per cent of all cats observed gave birth after the 65th day, and 13 per cent before the 63rd day.

If the average period of 53 to 65 days is exceeded, there is no cause for concern, so long as it is possible to feel the kittens moving in the mother's uterus and the cat behaves normally and takes food. Pregnant and nursing cats require an improved diet, richer in protein, mineral salts and vitamins than normal, and as pregnancy proceeds the cat will probably demand larger quantities. It is probably better to give more frequent small meals than to allow the cat to overload its gastro-intestinal tract by gorging. The more varied the diet at this time, the better the effect on the offspring. Up to a teaspoonful of bonemeal may be mixed in with the daily food or calcium tablets given. If the cat should be constipated at this time, a teaspoon of medicinal paraffin should be added to the food every second day. Exercise is the best antidote. The mammary glands usually only enlarge shortly before the birth of the litter. However, a veterinary surgeon or a skilled breeder may be able to feel the foetuses, or embryos, through the abdominal wall after the fourth week.

Besides the 'Pill' for women, a 'pill' for dogs and cats has existed for some time now. Certain medications prescribed by the veterinary surgeon can prevent the cat from coming into season. However this is not without its complications. It can cause or exacerbate inflammation of the ovaries or the uterus. Such treatment should in any case only be used occasionally and not be given routinely. A better, if final, solution is to have the queen spayed. The neutering of a tom is even simpler, and requires scarcely any additional treatment. (See the chapter on cat ailments.)

If one day an entirely unexpected litter is born, and the owner of the mother has no interest whatsoever in keeping the kittens, as a true animal lover the kindest measure to adopt is to have them painlessly destroyed immediately. Kittens that are given away to people unknown to the owner of the mother cat, simply in order to be rid of them, mostly meet with a sad and uncertain fate, which may spell lifelong torment for the animal concerned. In such circumstances a veterinary surgeon will undertake to put the kittens to death painlessly. For older kittens or an adult cat, the surest and best method is for the veterinary surgeon to inject an overdose of anaesthetic. Trying to kill the kittens by drowning or hitting them on the head is unnecessary and cruel.

If the entire litter is destroyed this may cause galactostasis in the mother and lead to inflammation of the nipples. However, this tends to happen only if the kittens have already been suckling for some time. Cool compresses will sometimes help alleviate the condition.

Unwanted offspring

186

The pregnant cat behaves very differently depending on her character and temperament and the amount of trust she has in her owner. There is also a great difference between a cat undergoing a first pregnancy and an experienced mother cat. Some cats will become very closely attached to their owner during this time, and will want them to be present at the birth, others prefer to remain undisturbed and bring their kittens into the world unassisted, without complications. Yet another type of cat, particularly one used to living free, such as a farmyard cat, will withdraw into some secret dark corner, and will only return to her usual haunt some time later with the entire brood of kittens.

As a rule, it is most important to find the right place for the litter to be housed. The mother usually favours a semi-dark place, free of draughts and not too visible. The basket or kitten box should neither be too small, nor too big. During labour, the cat likes to push against the edge. The box should be prepared several days before the kittens are due, so that the prospective mother may become familiar with it. The underlay should not be too hard, and should be easy to clean. The kittens are completely helpless at first so, in order to prevent them from rolling out, the deepest part of the nest should always be the centre. The most successful arrangement has proved to be an underlay of soft straw or hay covered with several layers of newspaper, which are covered by a clean cloth, then several more layers of newspaper placed on top of this, finally topped with another clean piece of cloth to prevent slipping. With long-haired cats, which stand shortly before giving birth, the secretion that collects on the nipples may be carefully removed with a clean flannel dipped in warmed oil. It may otherwise harden and form a painful clot. If the cat does not remove her own stomach hairs around the nipples, possibly using them to line the nest, assistance may be given by using scissors. This facilitates the suckling of the newborn kittens, and avoids uncomfortable matting of the coat by the remains of milk.

Shortly before giving birth, most queens will stop eating altogether. Fresh water and milk are all that should continue to be given. The queen becomes noticeably more restless than usual. Labour-like contractions can occur as much as several days, or even a full week, beforehand without this having any detrimental implication. These contractions soon pass off again.

Approximately 24 hours before birth, the embryos descend towards the pelvis. The first labour pains may be expected about one hour before birth. Since the amniotic fluid is often licked up right away, this stage may easily be missed. If the labour pains continue for more than four hours without any visible progress being made, the veterinary surgeon should be consulted.

Beginning of parturition The cat's labour is clearly divided into the preparatory early stage, which serves to open the uterus and dilate the cervix, and the subsequent expulsive labour pains reinforced by abdominal muscular pressure, which precede the actual delivery. The labour can be very accurately charted. The cat mostly lies stretched out full length on her side, preferably pushing against the rim of the box or basket with her paws. The intervals between the individual contractions diminish all the time. Beginning with about two per phase, they increase to seven or eight, which follow each other in rapid succession. Some cats, especially inexperienced ones, make for the toilet tray at the onset of contractions, and adopt the posture for defecating, the stimulation of the contractions presumably being similar to the urge to defecate. More frequently the cat remains stretched out on her side and massages her stomach and sexual parts by licking. A few cats give birth in a crouching position. In a normal birth, everything is best left to the prospective mother, intervention being avoided. Help is very seldom necessary, since cats give birth with comparative ease.

Delivery will extend over a period ranging from half an hour to six hours. Even births lasting more than 12 hours have been completed uneventfully.

Usually the individual kittens are born at intervals of 15 to 30 minutes, although intervals of two hours can still be normal.

The stage of expulsion   The stage of expulsion of each kitten lasts no more than three minutes; 60 per cent of kittens born come into the world head first. Breech presentations are rarer, and are often attended by other complications. The newborn kittens are mostly still enveloped in the foetal membrane, which the mother cat opens as she bites through the umbilical cord. The cat immediately licks the kitten, thereby stimulating its respiration and circulation. The cat then drags out the afterbirth attached to the umbilical cord. Since the cat is a multiparous mammal, each foetus arrives with its own afterbirth. It is almost always eaten. As the cat does so, or even before, she bites through the umbilical cord. Young, inexperienced cats sometimes eat so much of the umbilical cord that they damage the newborn kitten's abdomen. A kitten injured in this way must be put to death. The mother will often appear to be quite rough with the newborn kittens, and their first attempts to cry can be heard. This rough handling has a very positive purpose—to fill the lungs with sufficient air.

After the birth   After these first essential measures have been completed, the kitten is thoroughly licked dry all over. This conduct is vital, since it is of the utmost significance in establishing the right mother–child relationship. This is also the time when the first contact noises are uttered. If the newborn kitten is removed from the box, it will immediately begin to utter cries of abandonment which prompt the mother to go in search.

If only one kitten is born it is usually rather large. A single birth is consequently almost always a difficult birth. Healthy newborn kittens will instinctively immediately search for the source of nourishing milk. If a kitten should lose its way in the attempt, and begin to cry, the mother will seize it by the neck, and put it in the right place. Eight nipples provide the kittens' nourishment.

My own experience with regard to the question of whether one should leave other cats or even the tom in the room where the birth is taking place, makes me give a very firm affirmative answer. Of course, the cats must know each other and have lived together previously.

Immediately after the birth, and in the case of a long-drawn-out labour at intervals during the birth, the cat should be offered warm milk, to which an egg-yolk may be added.

Short-haired cats usually produce larger litters than Persians. The size of the litter is on average between five and seven kittens. Siamese, in particular, are known for having large litters, as many as seven or eight. Litters of only one kitten are twice as common in Persians as in Siamese.

Newborn kittens normally weigh between 80 and 120 g ($2\frac{3}{4}$–$4\frac{1}{4}$ oz). The average weight is 105 g ($3\frac{3}{4}$ oz), the extremes being 50 g ($1\frac{3}{4}$ oz) and 140 g (5 oz). The rate of weight increase is on average about 100 g ($3\frac{1}{2}$ oz) per week, with extremes of 50 g ($1\frac{3}{4}$ oz) and 130 g ($4\frac{1}{2}$ oz). The normal weight at the end of the second month is between 1,000 and 1,300 g (35–46 oz). From the third month onwards young tom kittens gradually seem to overtake their sisters in their rate of weight increase. Adult toms weigh between 3.5 and 5.0 kg ($7\frac{1}{2}$–11 lb), queens between 3.5 and 4.0 kg ($7\frac{1}{2}$–9 lb).

Complications Although the majority of all cat births proceed unassisted and without complications, it is necessary to provide a little insight into the assistance that can be given by a cat's 'midwife'.

Simply insufficient or visibly decreasing contractions could indicate that intervention is required and that it is best to consult a veterinary surgeon.

If the labour appears to be following a normal course but after six hours there is no sign of a birth, a veterinary surgeon should be called in. The sudden discharge of amniotic fluid may dissuade you from calling for immediate assistance but if still nothing happens it will be needed. Some queens, especially first-time mothers, do not have a fully developed maternal instinct, and may consequently lack interest in their newborn kittens. They do not release the foetus from the foetal membrane, if there is one, they do not bite through the umbilical cord and they do not lick the kittens dry. If the kitten is still enveloped in the amniotic sac, this should be torn away with the utmost speed, and the nose and mouth wiped clean of mucus. In so doing, the kitten's head should be held downwards, so that any amniotic fluid that may have accumulated can drain away. If the umbilical cord needs to be severed, the cord should be squeezed approximately 5 cm away from the body, tied and then cut above the ligature with scissors sterilised in boiling water. Inflammation of the cord in a newborn kitten can result in death. Immediately after birth, bacillae can still enter by way of the umbilical cord. The kitten will stop suckling, become listless, and hours later die of blood poisoning. Prevention is the most important factor in this instance. Nest and cloths, scissors and thread, even the hands, must be absolutely sterile. The navel of the newborn kitten should be dabbed with antiseptic tincture.

False pregnancy As with humans, and other mammals, false pregnancies do occasionally occur in house cats. Cats that live an isolated existence shut away in a flat and kept well away from all other cats, only being brought to a stud tom for pairing for the briefest period, are especially prone to this phenomenon. If such an all-too-brief encounter results in pairing without conception, it may quite frequently result in a false pregnancy. Accompanied by all the symptoms of a normal pregnancy, it may last for four to six weeks or even for the full gestation period. The queen does not come into season again during this period. Her stomach swells, the nipples and milk develop, and the hormones react as in a normal pregnancy. Real contractions may even occur. Many cat owners have been fooled in this way. Blue Persians and Siamese are supposed to be particularly inclined to this. Cats with

189

false pregnancies have even been known to simulate suckling and nursing over a lengthy period, dragging woollen cloths and similar objects into their quarters as substitute kittens. Queens with false pregnancies may be used successfully as foster mothers for orphaned kittens. The cause of the false pregnancies appears to be a hormonal error, which can be triggered by certain environmental conditions. As much exercise as possible and plenty of distraction are the best therapy. The milk should not be drawn off. If it does not naturally dry up hormone treatment may be necessary.

The mother cat will probably welcome a bowl of water near the delivery box and may want to eat. In the days after giving birth she may be quite hungry as she has to produce milk for her kittens. Calcium, vitamins and cod-liver oil should be added to her food from time to time. For the first few days, the feeding dish should be placed right next to the basket, as the mother does not like leaving her kittens. If the tom is there, he may bring the queen food.

The newborn kittens are just like nestlings. They are still quite undeveloped. Their coat is not yet fully grown, the eyes are shut, they have no teeth, and they have great difficulty in performing even the most uncoordinated crawling movements. Above all, they are not yet thermostable, that is to say they are not yet capable of regulating their own body temperature and keeping it stable. This is why the warm proximity of the mother and a sheltered, warm breeding box are so essential.

Suckling   The kittens suckle for approximately four to eight weeks, and in the case of a large litter or poor milk supply, supplementary feeding should be started at about the fourth week (see section on feeding kittens) and certainly if they begin to show an interest in their mother's food. In the early period the newborn kittens display a curious rhythmical waggling of the head from side to side—which is an instinctive searching movement for the nipple. As they suckle, the kittens perform a rhythmic 'kneading' with their paws to stimulate the flow of milk. This instinctive movement is retained in later life. Even the adult cat will perform this kind of 'kneading' motion on a soft seat or lap.

Sometimes poor milk flow or infection during lactation can produce inflammation of the nipples. The nipple becomes swollen, red, hot and sensitive. The cat's general health is affected to a greater or lesser degree. Raised temperature, loss of appetite and apathy appear. At this point the veterinary surgeon should be urgently consulted.

The newborn period   The kitten is considered newborn from the first to the 15th day of its life. Hunger, a drop in the environmental temperature or even excessive heat will cause the newborn kitten distress and make it squeak. These squeaks, in a variety of pitches, are uttered immediately after birth, and will be frequently heard during the next 20 days. Individual sounds usually follow each other in rapid succession to make a noise sequence. The mouth opens as the kitten emerges. Whimpering sounds are the stimuli that make the mother carry a straying kitten back to its box. But growling, spitting and squeals may already be observed during this period. From about the fourth week onwards it is possible to detect the occasional irritated snarling. Since the kitten cannot hear until about the second week, mutual exchange of feelings with the mother is not possible until then.

190

The eyes open between the 9th and the 12th days. At birth the upper and the lower eyelids are firmly attached to each other. Not until the development of the epidermis is complete, do the lids separate. It is quite wrong and dangerous to interfere in the natural process. If considerably more than 12 days have passed, without the lids opening, then they may be dabbed with lukewarm water. Even once the eyes are open, the kittens cannot see right away. A further two to three days pass before they react to a source of light, and they do not respond to movement until after the 15th to 20th day of life. Likewise between the 9th and the 12th day, they attempt, still in a very wobbly fashion, to stand, walk and hop. From the second week on, they make their first pathetic attempts to scratch behind their ears. However, their lack of balance repeatedly defeats them. They also practise shaking their heads, stretching themselves, raking the dirt after performing their toilet and lashing their tails. Depending on the kitten's condition, the milk teeth appear in a particular order. The incisors appear between the 10th and 16th day, the canines between the 14th and 25th day, and the back teeth between the 21st and 60th day. There was even the case of a Siamese tom which did not complete its full set of milk teeth until it was 130 days old. However the milk teeth are usually all complete by about the eighth week. At between five and six months the milk teeth are shed and the permanent teeth begin to appear. They are fully out by between seven and nine months. The soreness of their gums at this time may make the kittens go off their food.

The mother cat has a very interesting, instinctive method of carrying her kittens, in order to bring a straying kitten back to the breeding box, or when the time comes to change their sleeping accommodation. She grips the kitten by the skin at the back of its neck with her teeth, and lifts it from the ground. As she does so, the kitten immediately goes limp, and hangs as if lifeless in its mother's grip. This is a defence mechanism, to prevent the kitten being hurt by its mother's teeth, while being carried.

First response to environment At some time during the third week, the kitten is able to see its mother and its brothers and sisters. Unlike those animals that must become mobile very rapidly, such as sheep, goats, horses and cattle, whose vision is developed within the first few hours, in cats and dogs, sight develops comparatively late and this is connected with the late development of the necessary sensory organs.

191

Scratching behind the ear is achieved in a manner characteristic of cats, and the kitten gradually explores and masters its surroundings. From the fourth week onwards we can observe the first attempts at play, initially still very hesitant and clumsy. The first attempts at climbing are made. Gradually the mother reduces the amount of immediate care she devotes to the kittens, and she also stops removing their excreta and urine. This is linked to their being partially weaned from an all-fluid diet.

Young kittens play a great deal. They can be observed almost always enacting games that reflect the real-life behaviour of adult cats. Prey-catching games alternate with fighting and taking-flight games. The kittens lie in wait for each other, plunge on top of one another, attack their mother's tail, and every moving object that attracts their attention is caught as a 'prey'. It is very seldom, only when the kittens have gone really too far, that the mother snaps at them or cuffs them gently with a paw. By about the 47th day, the kittens are able to wash their faces exactly like an adult cat. In general, all inborn forms of behaviour, apart from the sexual cycle, are fully developed by the time the kittens are 70 days old.

The family is usually split up when the mother's milk dries up. The number of kittens in the litter is obviously the determining factor in this. Larger litters of up to five or six kittens split up after six months, whereas smaller ones with only two or three kittens may remain together for up to eight months. Eventually the sharp teeth of the kittens become a nuisance to the mother cat, and she drives them off or tries to keep out of their way. Single kittens will often continue to suckle for a very long time, even when the mother no longer has any milk. Such kittens are best removed from the cat. A kitten is able to eat on its own at the age of about six weeks.

Hand-rearing

Newborn kittens which lose their mother through some mishap, must be hand-reared. This will also be necessary should the mother have no milk. If the kittens are constantly restless and squeaking, then the mother's milk supply should be tested. A suitable animal foster mother, or failing that, human help, must replace the mother. The most appropriate substitute is another mother cat, but it will be very rare to find one available at the required time. Even small dogs could be considered. It is important that the ages of the foster mother's own litter should be the same as that of the kittens that need fostering. Rubbing the kittens with the foster mother's scent, either with her milk, or if need be even with her urine, is of considerable help if they are to be adopted without fuss.

Bottle-rearing   Bottle-rearing is simpler, if not exactly an unmixed delight. For the first two weeks the kittens must be bottle-fed night and day at least every two hours. Keeping the kittens clean is most important, and they should be given gentle body massage with a soft cloth to stimulate the digestion. The composition of the milk is very important for artificially raised kittens. Cat's milk, apart from its 82 per cent water content, is composed of 3.3 per cent to 4.9 per cent fat, 7.1 per cent to 9.1 per cent protein, 4.9 per cent lactose and 0.6 per cent ash, and consequently is very similar to cow's or goat's milk, except for the higher protein content. Cow's milk contains almost 6 per cent more water. It would be most beneficial for the kittens if they could receive the colostrum, with its especially high protein, fat, mineral salt, vitamin and natural immunity content,

147/148   As the time for kittening approaches a cat's pregnancy will be clearly visible in her increase in girth.

149   A cat may produce enough milk to feed her kittens until they are ten weeks old, or for even longer, but they should be weaned much earlier.

192

154 *It always seems to be time for a wash, either for mother herself or for one of her litter.*

155 *What is going on? Mother's paw goes out to restrain her kitten from leaving her side.*

150   *A mother cat carries her kitten in her mouth gripping it by the loose skin on the back of its neck.*

151   *Although watched over by their mother these kittens do not seem to trust the photographer. The angle of the ears of the two looking at the camera suggests that they are very much on guard.*

152   *A new hiding place is always an exciting discovery. To the wild cat it could be a safe haven, to the pet a new place to play hide and seek.*

153   *Three-week-old Seal point Siamese kittens*

154 *It always seems to be time for a wash, either for mother herself or for one of her litter.*

155 *What is going on? Mother's paw goes out to restrain her kitten from leaving her side.*

156 *This Siamese kitten is growing rapidly, its mother may soon have to part with it. Kittens should not be taken to their new homes until they are least 8 and preferably 10–12 weeks old.*

157 A Tortoiseshell and white shorthair with her kitten: known by many in the United States as a Calico cat, this is a variety which is almost invariably female.

158/159 Hey, mother! How about another game? No, keep still. It's bath-time once again.

160/161/162 From an early age, kittens like these Tabby longhairs enjoy a fighting game, learning to develop coordination and skills which they may use in earnest later.

163 *A Silver tabby longhair kitten*

164 *This pretty kitten does not belong
to any particular breed. Its wickerwork
carrying basket opens at the top making
it much easier to lift the cat in and out
than types that open at the side.*

165/166/167 This litter of Siamese kittens includes both Lilac point and Seal point. They have already developed the elegant wedge-shaped head of the breed but their masks and points are only palely suggested and will spread and darken with pencil lines of colour connecting the central facial colour with the bottom of the ears.

168 A vantage point in the sunshine from which to keep an eye on everything is what every kitten wants. This one looks as though it is not going to miss a thing.

169/170 Playing and fighting has ruffled and tousled the fur of the Blue longhair kittens and they would benefit from grooming. Even kittens' coats should be kept in good condition and early grooming will quickly get them used to being handled.

171 No one should take on a kitten
unless he is prepared to give it proper
care and breeders should investigate
potential owners to make sure that
they are suited to the responsibility that
looking after a cat entails.

which the mother cat produces 24 hours after delivery. This milk which provides the kittens with resistance to disease and maintains their health, is very important during the first few days of life. Since the kitten should retain the natural sucking posture when drinking it should be held on the lap or in the crook of the arm. The head should never be bent back, nor should the kitten be placed on its back, because of the danger of choking and suffocation.

For the first few days, only a doll's feeding bottle should be used, since the teat would otherwise be far too big. Even a non-fluffy handkerchief dipped in milk could be used. The milk must be kept at a temperature of 38°C (100°F). Keeping the bottle in a saucepan of warm water helps to keep the temperature constant from beginning to end. The hole in the teat of the bottle should not be so big that the milk runs out by itself, as there is then the danger that the milk might go down the kitten's windpipe, which might result in its death from aspiration pneumonia. To begin with the kitten will drink little but often. Left-over milk should not be re-used.

After three weeks of bottle feeding, it is worth trying to change over to a meat diet. Tiny lumps of meat should be put through the mincer and warmed to body temperature. Each kitten should be given at most two lumps to begin with. On the third day the first feed of egg-milk in the morning could be replaced, and the last feed before sleeping could consist of a teaspoonful of minced meat.

Gradually the dish should replace the bottle, in order to reduce the work load a little. Until the kittens are six weeks old, they will need six to seven meals per day.

Stately, kindly, lordly friend
Condescend
Here to sit by me, and turn
Glorious eyes that smile and burn,
Golden eyes, love's lustrous meed,
On the golden page I read.

All your wondrous wealth of hair
Dark and fair,
Silken-shaggy, soft and bright
As the clouds and beams of night,
Pays my reverent hand's caress
Back with friendlier gentleness.

Dogs may fawn on all and some
As they come;
You, a friend of loftier mind,
Answer friends alone in kind.
Just your foot upon my hand
Softly bids it understand.

The Birman breed, perhaps the result of carefully planned mixed breeding between a Siamese and a solid-coloured longhair, was recognised in France in 1925 but was not recognised in Britain and America until the mid-1960s. Its exact origins are uncertain. There are various accounts, some of which maintain that the Birman came from Buddhist temples in Burma. It is longer-bodied and longer in the nose than the standard longhair, so perhaps it may come of different long-haired stock, while colouring, medium size, long body and smooth nose are Siamese characteristics. The colour of the Birman is ivory with the contrasting brownish-black or blue points of the Siamese. The most unusual feature is that the four paws are white, ending in an even line, with the white on the sole of the rear paws coming to a point, to form a 'glove'. Birman kittens are white all over. Crossing with solid-coloured Persians does not improve Birmans.

The Colourpoint, or Himalayan as it is known in America, looks very similar and is a definite cross-breed carefully created to introduce the Siamese coat pattern into a long-haired cat. Originally bred in the United States in the course of genetic experiments it was subsequently bred in England in the three Siamese colours with the coat and type of the longhair. Today several different colour varieties are recognised under Standard 13b Colourpoint: including Seal point, Blue point, Chocolate point, Red point and Lilac point. This long-haired cat was first given breed status in the mid-1950s and quickly found many admirers. Pure-breeding requires extremely careful selection in order to suppress the Siamese body-type. The most difficult trait to produce is the bright, clear, deep blue eyes required by the standard. Colourpoint kittens, too, are solid white. The body should be cobby, the legs low. A short, bushy tail is desirable: in no case must it be pointed. The head should be large and round, any Siamese-type trait is considered a fault. The face and nose should be short for preference. The well-tufted ears, spaced wide apart, should be very bushy. The deep blue eyes are large, round and wide open.

Breeds of mixed origin with short- and long-haired ancestry

210

In contrast to the two preceding breeds the Balinese, recognised in America since 1963 and well on the way to recognition in Britain, is a Siamese cat with long fur. It is not a cross with a longhair but has developed from mutant long-haired cats that occasionally appear in Siamese litters.

One of the oldest breeds in America, the Maine Coon cat is thought to be a cross between the original short-haired type imported by the early colonists and a longhair of Angora type, for it has a smaller, sharper head than the other longhairs. It is only known in America, and especially on the eastern seaboard.

Another development in America and Australia is the Cameo cat, an introduction of red colouring to the Smoke and Chinchilla type of longhair. It has a pure white coat overlaid by a coat with red ticking, now recognised in three colour strengths: Shell, Shaded and Smoke going from most pale to darkest. There is also a Tabby cameo with red tabby markings but in other varieties tabby markings would be a fault.

More new breeds There have been quite a number of other attempts to produce new forms of long-haired cat from established short-haired types. There is the Somali, a long-haired version of the Abyssinian, the Cymric, a long-haired Manx, and Chocolate and Lilac longhairs have also been produced.

Among the shorthairs the most noticeable of recent breeds is the Egyptian Mau, or the Foreign Spotted as it is known in Britain where it has now been recognised. This was a conscious attempt to produce a cat which would look like some of the spotted cats in Ancient Egyptian paintings. The American strain was developed from cats which actually came from Cairo but British breeders made use of spotted cats which occurred in the breeding of the Tabby-point Siamese. The American standard requires a less oriental type than the British where an added refinement has been to produce a scarab-like mark upon the cat's forehead and between its ears like the beetle symbols which were such a feature of Egyptian art.

Among foreign types some American organisations recognise an Albino Siamese and one may also come across the Tonkinese, a solid brown Siamese produced by crossings with Burmese or Havanas, and the Ocicat, rather similar to the Mau with spotted coat and limited tabby markings which has been produced in two shades of chestnut.

Two totally new hair types have also been produced in America: the Wirehair, developed from a chance mutation, which is identical with the Domestic shorthair except for its medium-length stiff coat, and the Exotic shorthair, recognised since 1967 which is a cross between the longhair and the Domestic shorthair giving a Persian-looking cat but with a shorter coat now recognised in all the longhair colours, but not in Peke-faced.

Ink and brush drawing by Joseph Hegenbarth

John Gay   The Old Women and Her Cats

A wrinkled hag, of wicked fame
Beside a little smoky flame
Sat hov'ring, pinched with age and frost;
Her shrivell'd hands, with veins embossed.
About her swarm'd a num'rous brood
Of Cats, who lank with hunger mew'd.
Teaz'd with their cries her choler grew,
And thus she sputter'd. Hence, ye crew.
Fool that I was to entertain
Such imps, such fiends, a hellish train!
Had ye been never hous'd and nurs'd
I, for a witch, had ne'er been curs'd.
To you I owe, that crowds of boys
Worry me with eternal noise;

Straws laid across my pace retard,
The horse-shoe's nail'd (each threshold's guard).
The stunted broom the wenches hide,
For fear that I should up and ride.

Replies a Cat. Let's come to proof.
Had we ne'er starved beneath your roof
We had, like others of our race,
In credit liv'd, as beasts of chase.
'Tis infamy to serve a hag;
Cats are thought imps, her broom a nag;
And boys against our lives combine,
Because, 'tis said, your cats have nine.

Cat ailments

**Basic rules
for treating
sick cats**

Just as with any other animal, by the time a cat is visibly unwell, things have already reached a fairly advanced stage. One should never, therefore, hesitate to take an obviously sick cat to the veterinary surgeon.

Cats are very susceptible to disorders of the internal organs. Only in a minority of cases, where the illness is very slight and the cause readily identifiable, is it advisable for the owner to treat the cat himself.

Symptoms   The first general sign of an illness is a change in behaviour. A cat that is normally trusting, will suddenly become timid and seek out some dark, sheltered corner. The cat becomes noticeably weaker and in need of sleep. It refuses food; even favourite titbits fail to tempt it. The cat neglects its personal grooming; the coat becomes dull and lifeless, often standing out from the body, and looking unkempt and dishevelled. A healthy cat always has a silky-soft, smooth and lustrous coat.

The eyes, too, show very plainly what condition the animal is in. The healthy cat has clear, moist and bright eyes. The opposite must be a serious warning. It is not often that the third eyelid, or nictitating membrane comes across the eyes. If it does this is usually an external indication of some disorder. If the cat shows any of the symptoms described here, a veterinary surgeon should be consulted immediately. Delay or the use of a home remedy is only likely to make the condition spread and deteriorate. The body temperature of the cat is significant. If a veterinary surgeon is consulted, he is very likely to inquire what the animal's temperature is.

Taking the temperature   To take the cat's temperature, use a heavy glass thermometer. Shake it down and grease the narrower end with skin cream. Then insert the thermometer carefully some 3 cm ($1\frac{1}{8}$ in) into the rectum, do not push hard but rotate it gently in. Leave it for at least three minutes. If the patient remains undisturbed and

213

readily permits this procedure, then one person can manage alone. However, with a restless animal or in unfamiliar surroundings such as a clinic, it is better for two people to be at hand. The person the animal is most used to should hold it down on the table by the neck and in the lumbar region, while a second person should hold the tail and slightly lift the hindquarters. If no second person is available to help, and the cat is uncooperative, wrap it in a blanket, to prevent scratching, so that only the head and tail are free. Only then can its temperature be taken relatively safely.

The normal temperature of a domestic cat is between 38 °C and 39.5 °C (100 °F–103 °F). Kittens usually have a temperature of approximately 39 °C (102 °F).

It should be taken into account that the upset of this kind of unaccustomed handling may in itself be enough to raise the body temperature temporarily. In order to be sure, the temperature should be taken again later, when the initial disturbance has died down.

There are also normal physiological fluctuations within the course of the day, just as with human beings. Body temperature is likewise affected, if only minimally, by age, sex and psychological factors.

The pulse of the cat is taken on the inside of the thigh, where it can be strongly felt. The normal frequency of the pulse is between 100 and 120 beats per minute. With kittens, the frequency is marginally higher at 130 to 140, and with young cats it is already steadier at between 110 and 130. Normal respiration is from 20 to a maximum of 40 breaths per minute. Like temperature, frequency of pulse and breathing are affected by psychological factors such as excitement and anxiety. If the body temperature is found to exceed 39.5 °C (103 °F), the cat should be taken to the veterinary surgeon immediately. It will usually be found to be suffering from an infectious illness.

Minor illnesses How can we recognise minor illnesses, which we can treat ourselves, if the occasion arises? One diagnostic aid that should not be overlooked is the cat's stool or motion. Normally its consistency is semi-soft. A single slight deviation from this norm is not necessarily significant.

Slight diarrhoea is usually the result of the wrong food or unsuitable stolen food. The composition of the cat's recent diet should be carefully analysed, and corrected if necessary. Missing out a meal or two may solve the problem. Avoid feeding liver, kidney or other offal, beef or milk. Try to get the cat to swallow a little kaolin and offer it chicken, fish, rice and cabbage if it will eat them. The disorder is usually quickly cured, provided

214

there is not a more serious underlying cause. However, in obstinate cases, persisting more than a couple of days, or if the condition deteriorates coupled with other symptoms of illness, the veterinary surgeon should be consulted immediately, since many dangerous illnesses begin with diarrhoea.

Constipation frequently occurs and can usually be traced to the wrong kind of diet, and often to a lack of exercise or a placid temperament, as for example in neutered cats. The belly may be slightly distended. The cat will frequently try to defecate but without success. Initially the animal is restless, and later becomes apathetic. The first step in trying to produce a result, is to feed the cat with raw liver. The fat content of the milk ration should be increased by adding cream or condensed milk, or raw fish or raw marrow may be offered. One teaspoonful of salad oil or a glycerin suppository introduced at the other end, should usually do the trick. There is no harm, either, in giving a teaspoonful of pure medicinal paraffin oil. Cats love licking the pure vegetable oil from sardine tins. Castor oil, however, is distinctly harmful. Laxatives prescribed for human use should never be given to cats.

As a rule, cats tend to vomit very easily. This is by no means a sign of illness. Just taking cold or excessively fatty food can make them vomit. When several domestic cats are kept together they tend to bolt their food greedily and too hastily. In these cases, the cats will often vomit and then eat up what they have brought up. The mother will sometimes vomit partially-digested food for her kittens to eat. This does not count as genuine vomiting. However, this somewhat unpleasant behaviour can also appear in cases of persistent constipation, gastro-intestinal inflammation, worm infestation, poisoning, because of the presence of foreign bodies or as a result of infectious disease.

If the vomiting becomes more frequent, and is combined with other symptoms of illness, if it has a brownish or greenish colour or contains streaks of blood, then the veterinary surgeon should be consulted without further delay. Normal vomiting, however, occurs after eating grass (see the chapters on diet and grooming) and is more common with long-haired cats, being simply a means of ridding the animal of troublesome hairs, which have entered the stomach as a result of grooming, or of getting rid of the indigestible remains of prey the cat has caught for itself.

The seriousness of sickness resulting from chills is very difficult to assess. Cats are very sensitive to draughts. If the cat, with its love of keeping warm, is too cosseted it will catch cold much more readily when the temperature changes or damp, cold weather sets in, than will a house cat accustomed to roaming freely out of doors. Light nasal catarrh with frequent sneezing, nose-scratching, an initially clear watery nasal discharge, which subsequently becomes thick and mucous, or conjunctivitis are symptoms that may develop. The eyes may be cleaned using a soft cloth soaked in warm water, or penicillin eye drops prescribed by the veterinary surgeon may be given. Such problems often clear up naturally quite quickly, but severe cases of nasal catarrh or conjunctivitis can be symptoms of severe infectious disease, and the veterinary surgeon should be consulted immediately.

Visiting the veterinary surgeon If it is necessary to consult a veterinary surgeon, he will
usually be a small mammals practitioner with an animal clinic, and the patient will

nearly always have to be taken there. Transporting a sick cat, however, is an easy undertaking. A carrying basket of the right size, preferably one that the cat has already been accustomed to using when well, a transport cage or a suitable wooden box are satisfactory. Briefcases or outsize handbags are considerably less suitable, since the cat may become very disturbed at the unfamiliarity of the surroundings and may break loose. Sick animals should, as far as possible, be spared any additional upset. They are very distrustful, easily excited and aggressive and even people who normally have the animal's complete confidence and love may, in such cases, suddenly be bitten and scratched for no reason whatever. The owner must at all events be prepared for such utterly uncharacteristic behaviour from the animal.

A closed room is essential for treating a sick cat. There should be the minimum of available nooks and hiding places for the cat to slip into. A fresh specimen of the patient's stool brought in a sterilised glass container is very valuable. A well-stocked home medicine chest specially for the cat, and clearly marked as such, is a worthwhile acquisition. It should contain an unbreakable thermometer, a pair of blunt-ended tweezers, blunt-ended scissors, plastic (disposable) syringes for administering medicine or liquid food, bandage gauze, plasters, kaolin, a universal antidote and such ointments and drugs as your veterinary surgeon suggests and will prescribe.

Administering medication and injections

If a cat owner is obliged to give his pet medication of any kind, he will usually soon run into difficulties. Only the rarest, most trusting of animals will accept unpalatable medicines and swallow them straight down. Attempts to slip a pill or some powder into a favourite dish for the cat to take are unlikely to meet with success. When ill, if it takes food at all, the cat usually chews every little morsel thoroughly at great length. This method may, however, work where a number of cats are all kept together, as sheer greed makes the animals swallow the food whole, without chewing it. An added refinement of this technique is to offer a number of morsels without any added medication, and only then to insert it. Valerian can be used to hide medication, since cats so love the smell of this drug, that they roll around on it, as if drunk. The most practical way is to wrap the cat firmly in a blanket, so that only the head remains free. Then, using thumb and middle finger, gently and carefully prise open the mouth and place the pill held in tweezers as far back as possible at the base of the tongue. Now shut the cat's mouth and stroke the throat a little, to stimulate it to swallow. To keep the mouth open, a well-rounded smooth stick such as a pencil, may also be used, this should be inserted carefully between the back teeth. No metal object should ever be used for this purpose, since the cat can easily break its teeth on it.

Liquid medicines may be administered with a dropper or, if the owner happens to possess one, with a plastic syringe inserted sideways between the rows of teeth or the medicine can be dribbled just into the pouch of the cheek. It is best to introduce the medicine a little at a time as this produces a better swallowing reflex than if it is released in an even steady stream. The head must be held horizontal to prevent choking. If the fluid is simply tipped into its opened mouth, the cat will very quickly choke, which may result in aspiration pneumonia. Occasionally, if it is simply a matter of a few drops of a

216

173/174/175 Colourpoint cats are known as Khmer cats in some parts of Europe but they have nothing to do with Cambodia being a breed created in Britain by introducing Siamese markings into long-haired cats. Their type should be as for other longhairs and not in the least oriental.

176   *A Blue point colourpoint*

177   *An adult cat's teeth should be regularly checked for the build up of tartar deposits. An inspection of the mouth may also help in diagnosing illness.*

178   *A skilled veterinary surgeon will feel the animal's abdomen to locate sources of pain and to discover swelling and other physical disorders.*

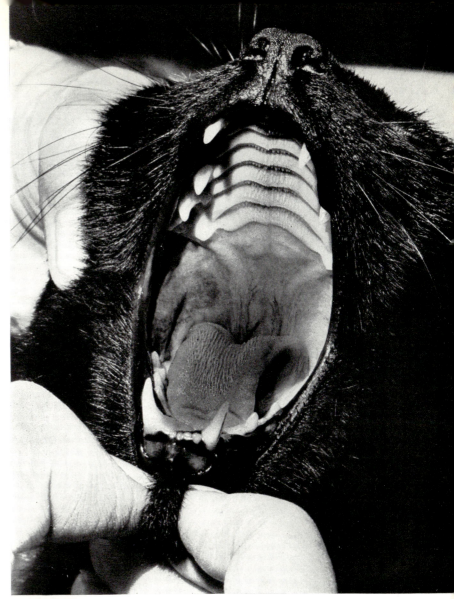

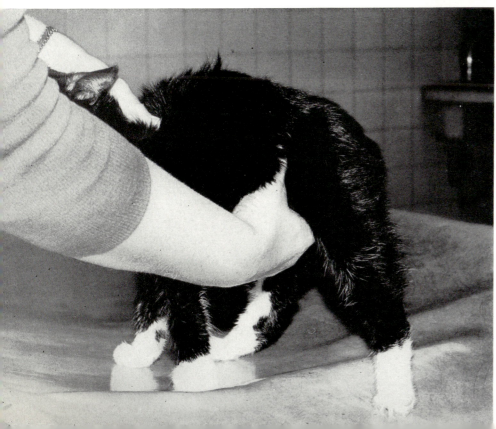

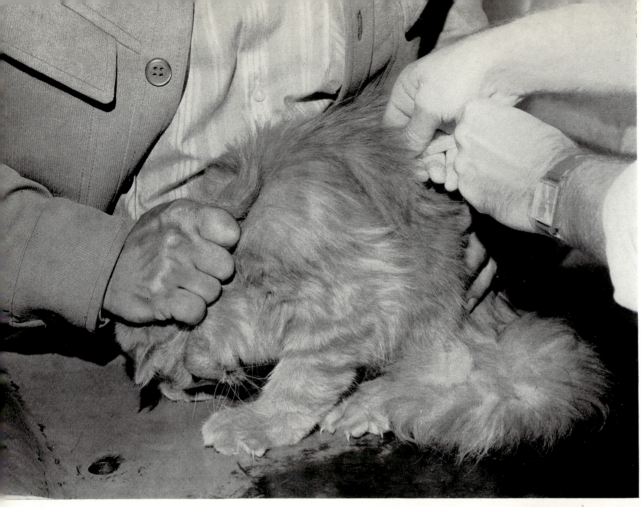

179 Subcutaneous injections, given into the tissue between the skin and muscle, are scarcely felt by most cats. They are often given into the loose skin of the neck. Injections may also be given into the muscle tissue or, in the case of anaesthetics or drugs requiring a high blood concentration, into the veins of the legs.

180 An unbreakable thermometer is lubricated and inserted into the cat's anus to take its body temperature.

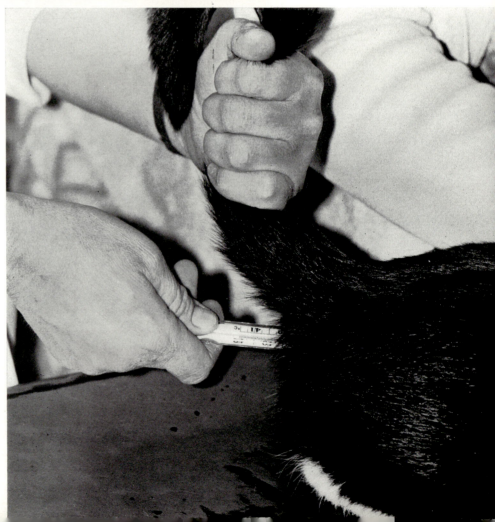

181 If you think a cat is ill do not delay in consulting the veterinary surgeon. It is wise to have a proper carrying box or basket but if you have to use a makeshift carrier ensure that the cat cannot scrabble its way out.

182 Eye medication is easily applied.

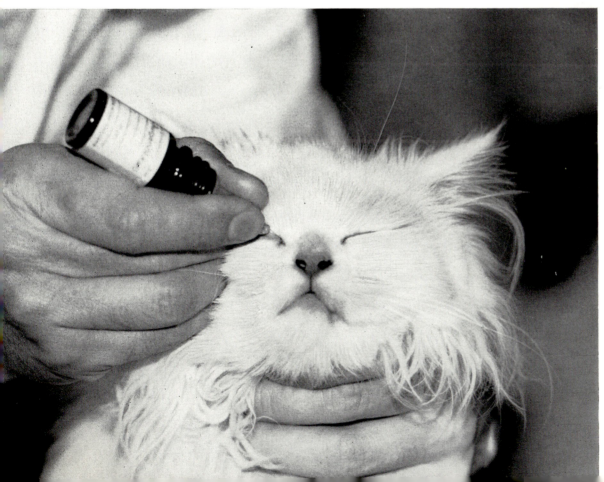

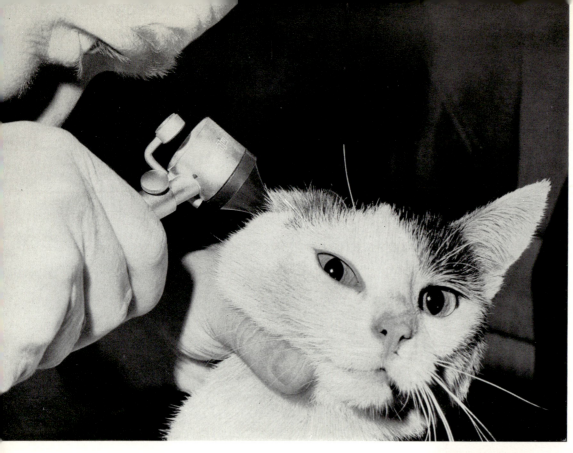

183 A cat's ears should always be kept clean and should be checked regularly for mites. Light infestations are usually easily treated but if ignored can take hold and seriously damage the cat's ears.

184 Some cats put up a great resistance to taking medicine. Gripping a cat around the throat certainly will not help. The head should be held still and the throat gently massaged to encourage swallowing after a small amount of fluid has been squeezed into the mouth with a syringe.

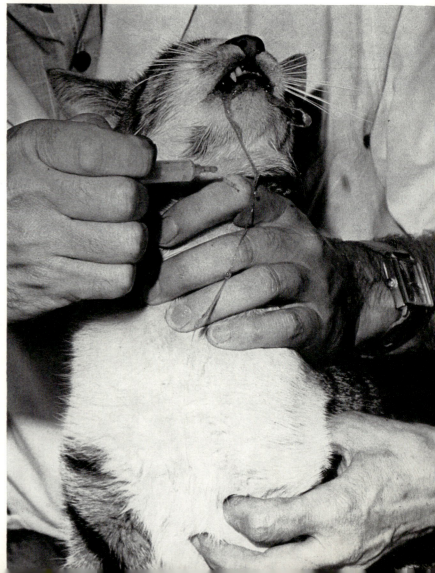

medicine, it is enough to drop the medicine on to the nose. A reflex will make the cat lick it off immediately with its tongue. If the exact amount is not important, as for example with vitamin drops, they can simply be dribbled on to the paw, which the fastidious cat will instantly lick clean.

Swallowing foreign bodies

Cats very easily swallow foreign bodies, such as bone splinters or fishbones with food, or needles, drawing pins, string, glass, buttons and the like while playing.

If the foreign body is still in the mouth, the throat, or at the top of the oesophagus, the symptoms are usually clear and unmistakable. Retching, coughing, heavy salivation, attacks of suffocation, miaowing and incessant wiping of the mouth with the paw are signs that appear with varying intensity depending on the degree of the disturbance. In simple cases where the cause is still clearly visible and recognisable, immediate help can be given. Splinters of bone or fishbones may have penetrated between the teeth or into the hard gum or have penetrated between the upper and lower teeth and the cheek or become wedged firm there. The animal should be tightly wrapped in a blanket, its mouth opened, if necessary a tongue depressor inserted and, using a pocket torch to illuminate the interior of the mouth and a pair of tweezers, the cause of distress may be carefully removed. In all other cases, where the cause of the trouble is no longer visible in the mouth enabling its easy removal, the veterinary surgeon should take over immediately. Needles, even complete with thread, are often swallowed by kittens in abandoned play. These often become lodged at the base of the tongue, in the pharynx and in the oesophagus, so that intervention by an unpractised hand may only make the animal's situation worse. Removal by surgery is usually unavoidable.

Essential surgery

In many kinds of illness, surgery is essential if the cat is to be restored to health. This will almost invariably involve the transportation of the patient to the veterinary surgeon.

After any kind of operation the cat requires the maximum rest and an undisturbed, soft, dark place for its accommodation. However, the patient should be kept under constant supervision, so that its condition can be monitored. Depending on the veterinary surgeon's instructions, the cat should be given a specially prescribed diet, or light food.

Rather than use its normal litter, cellular wadding or shredded absorbent kitchen paper are best for the litter tray of a newly-operated animal, to avoid getting the wound dirty. If the cat is restless, it may be necessary to fit a funnel-like paper collar around its neck to prevent it from licking or gnawing at any parts of its body.

Cats that are to be operated upon are first given a general anaesthetic, usually by injection. If the owner knows that this is to take place, he should see to it that the cat is brought to the clinic with an empty stomach, no food being given for eight hours previously. Tell the veterinary surgeon if it has eaten more recently as the animal might vomit during the operation, which could have fatal consequences. Since an anaesthetic produces a considerable drop in the body temperature, it is important to keep the cat as warm as possible after the operation. Surgery may become necessary on more or less any of the organs or parts of the body. Abscesses, ulcers and tumours must almost always be

225

removed by operation. Haematomas (a pronounced swelling due to the presence of a blood clot) in the ear are very common in cats. A marked inclination to shake its head following an operation, or the presence of mites in the ear will often result in the ear being banged against a hard object, causing bleeding. Haematomas are frequently caused by bites from other cats or from dogs. Eye injuries as a result of accidents or fights are not uncommon, and often an operation is the only course open. A cloudiness of the lens, known as cataract, can have a variety of causes, ranging from simple injury to tuberculosis, and may be congenital.

Sometimes a dental extraction will become necessary. Animals with a congenital cleft palate should not be allowed to breed, as this deformity would otherwise be continually passed on. Foreign bodies that have been absorbed will often require an operation to remove them, especially if they have become lodged in the oesophagus, in the stomach, or in the intestinal canal. Stomach ulcers are rare, but can be caused by hairballs. Difficult cases of prolapse of the rectum, visible as a round, bluish-red mass protruding from the anus, may result from severe constipation, enteritis or general weakness of the sphincter and frequently need surgical treatment. Stomach operations necessitated by the growth of tumours, or accidents, injuries sustained such as bites, or shot-gun wounds, are not uncommon. Surgery is essential in the case of suppurating inflammation of the female internal reproductive organs, such as the uterus. The unmistakable symptom of this kind of disorder is a brownish, or bloody purulent discharge from the vagina. The animal becomes listless and completely apathetic. Surgery may also be required in connection with kittening, for example if the foetuses are in the wrong position. In complicated cases, delivery by caesarian section may be necessary. Surgery may also be required to deal with the many different injuries that can result from accidents of every kind, as outlined in the following section.

Unfortunately, road accidents, as a result of which pet cats are injured, are by no means uncommon. If a cat is found lying in the street, severely injured as a result of a car accident, one should speak to it in soothing tones and try to get it to a veterinary surgeon with all possible speed, even if there is no outward sign of external injuries. An animal that is visibly wounded should preferably not be wrapped up but should be carried on a firm support. However, even the owner should be most careful in his handling of the injured animal, since it will be in a state of extreme excitation, and fear may well cause it to bite or scratch. It is first of all essential to make sure that its air passages are clear. Mouth and nose could be blocked by blood, mucus or fragments of tissue. If the cat is unconscious, its tongue should be drawn out of its mouth.

Falling from a height—from a tree, a balcony or a window—bites sustained from other cats or from dogs, gunshots and fighting may all cause injuries of many different kinds. Even burns are not uncommon in the home. An accident or fall often causes fractures. The cat is inclined to recover from slight fractures naturally and easily. In more complicated cases, however, the veterinary surgeon is likely to adopt treatment using such methods as plaster of Paris, zinc oxide dressing or splints. There are many instances of cats being put in plaster and left to rest quietly for many days, after which they were per-

Accidents and injuries

226

fectly all right again. To heal a complicated fracture, it may, however, sometimes be necessary to pin the bone. Care must be taken to ensure that the patient uses the litter tray as regularly as possible.

Injuries resulting from accidents   Inability to support weight on either one or both posterior limbs indicates a pelvic fracture. This frequently affects urinating and defecating. The veterinary surgeon will decide whether treatment other than absolute rest is necessary. Inhibited movement, cries of pain and a projection to one side of the thorax as well as marked abdominal respiration suggest a fractured rib. Rest and a bandage encircling the body are often enough to ensure recovery. If an accident or a fall cause internal haemorrhaging, for example from a tear in the liver, which manifests itself by symptoms of anaemia and rapid physical decline, then only rapid surgical intervention will save the animal, if it can be saved at all. If blood flows from the nose and mouth, becoming slightly frothy as the animal breathes out, a tear in the lungs is indicated. Unless the injury is minor, there is no hope for the animal.

If, after an accident, the cat shows marked unsteadiness when standing or walking, such as swaying, trembling, falling over and, in severe cases, vomiting and loss of consciousness, then it has suffered severe damage of the brain or spinal cord. Minor or severe concussion or contusion of the spinal cord cannot, however, be treated by surgery. Absolute quiet and rest, preferably in a darkened room, possibly with application of cold compresses to the cat's head and appropriate treatment with medication are indicated.

Bites   Fights between cats or between cats and dogs frequently result in injuries caused by biting or clawing. Fresh, gaping wounds must be stitched. Older wounds that have become infected and are suppurating must first be opened to drain the flow of pus. A cat owner may clean fresh wounds with clean water or a very dilute solution of hydrogen peroxide. Any hairs that may have entered the wound when the bite occurred, should be carefully removed with tweezers. The entire body of the cat, especially in the case of a longhair, should be carefully examined, since bite wounds are frequently hidden by the hairs being stuck together. They may not be discovered for days, by which time they will have become heavily infected and full of pus. Even with open wounds, the owner must beware lest the wound closes only on the surface; while suppuration is going on underneath, this infection may rapidly spread and become extremely dangerous.

In the case of bite wounds the 'other half' of the bite should be searched for, since the tooth marks made by both the upper and lower jaws are usually present. Tetanus infection of a wound very seldom occurs in cats. However, if it does, the symptoms become apparent after 8 to 14 days, when a muscular rigidity sets in; intense fear, gnashing of the teeth, closing of the nictitating membrane and clenching of the jaw are further symptoms of this dangerous infection.

Burns   Cats that spend most of their time in the home may suffer burns from radiators, cookers and electric current and scalding from hot fluids, and precautions should be taken to prevent this happening. A first-degree burn produces instant inflammation of the skin. Severe redness of the skin, hair standing up on end and some discharge of serum may be evident. The hair usually falls out from the burn area. Potato flour, boracic ointment or a similar proprietary ointment will soothe the pain.

227

A second-degree burn will produce immediate, severe blistering. The hair loss is considerable and may persist for years. Third-degree burns covering more than one-third of the body surface will cause death. General disorders, such as diarrhoea or blood-stained urine as a result of toxic absorption may all occur with first-, second- and partial third-degree burns.

Owners of sexually mature cats living in flats, especially in big cities, will very soon have to contend with the problem of the animal's sexual drive. The urge to roam, the nerve-shattering yowling that robs one of sleep, the offensive smells of the tom cat's spraying will rapidly lead to a discussion of the quickest possible solution of this problem.

One highly questionable, unreliable and only temporarily effective method is the prevention of ovulation by means of hormone injections. This will prevent the cat from coming into heat for about six months. Pedigree cats should, however, be closely watched for the reactions to these injections. Some cats will still come into season about two to three months after such injections, others not for nine months. It is, therefore, best to be on one's guard all the time. Furthermore the cat should be permitted to come into season normally once after each treatment to prevent any adverse effect on its general health.

A contraceptive pill, which has a similar effect to that used by humans, may be used for dogs and cats. The animal's receptivity is thereby postponed but not permanently so. So if, after a predetermined interval, the cat is taken off the pill, it can again come into season and have kittens. Recent findings have, however, shown that the pill is not entirely reliable. Apart from the fact that it is quite complicated to ensure that the cat takes the pill regularly at the appropriate time, in many cases side effects have occurred such as inflammation of the uterus.

With animals where breeding is no longer either desired or is impossible for health reasons, sterilisation or castration are advisable.

Sterilisation involves the tying of the fallopian tubes of the female, and the tying of the vas deferens in the tom. That is to say, they are made infertile, while retaining their sex drive, with all its accompanying inconvenient characteristics. With castration, how-ever, the testicles are removed from the tom, and with spaying, the ovaries are removed from the female. With this method of 'alteration' the sex drive disappears. Neutered, or altered, animals become more 'home-loving', cease to roam and become more attached to their owners. Neutered cats may become larger and are more likely to be-come fat, if overfed.

In principle, the operation to spay a female may be performed on the animal at any age, but the ideal age is between five and eight months.

Spaying involves the opening up of the abdomen. The cat must not be fed until it is fully recovered from the anaesthetic or it may vomit but it does not require any special diet. For some time after the operation, the animal must be kept especially clean.

Toms are best castrated at between five and seven months. The animals should be in sound health, and have neither internal nor external parasites. Older females and toms may also be neutered. However, hormonal production may still persist and the secondary symptoms of the sex drive abate only very gradually.

Intestinal parasites Cat lovers are often puzzled as to how such fastidiously clean house pets as cats can pick up worms. It may be some small comfort to learn that there is seldom a cat that does not have worms at some time. These intestinal parasites are known as endoparasites. By contrast with these, there are a number of different external parasites, known as ectoparasites, that live on the animal's body or in the upper skin layers.

Evidence of endoparasites Endoparasites of the intestines are by no means harmless, even if they only become really dangerous once they are present in large numbers. Once evidence of the presence of intestinal parasites has appeared advice should be sought from the veterinary surgeon, who will prescribe an appropriate worming agent. It is useful to bring the veterinary surgeon the stool containing any worm or tapeworm that has been passed, placing it in a clean glass container, so that he can make an immediate diagnosis. Examining a fresh motion, in which the worm eggs may also show up under the microscope, is a most valuable aid to diagnosis. Since, however, worms or their eggs are mostly passed periodically, the motions, preferably the morning ones, should be inspected on several successive days. Finding the motion free of worms on one occasion alone is no sure indication that none are present.

There is no point in selecting just any worming medicine. A specially prescribed medicine by the veterinary surgeon for this particular case should be given, and above all it is essential to follow the exact instructions as to the dosage. Some owners believe that fresh minced carrot or small amounts of garlic regularly included in the diet will ensure that a cat is kept relatively free of worms, although this has no medical backing.

The most striking signs, that will prompt us to consult the veterinary surgeon immediately, are a pot belly, accompanied by a distinct loss of weight, nervous, restless behaviour and loss of appetite. In some cases, however, the cat may have a voracious appetite. Worms can appear in the motions, be vomited, sneezed out or coughed up.

If the animal constantly licks its rear and slides along the floor or carpet on its bottom in a kind of 'tobogganing' movement, worm infestation may be indicated, but more often the cause is an inflammation of the anal sac or anal glands. Even though such an inflammation is not dangerous, the veterinary surgeon should still be consulted.

The types of intestinal parasites that occur in cats are: roundworms, tapeworms, hookworms, coccidiae, and trichinellae. Although it is not an intestinal parasite, liver fluke will also be included here.

Roundworms Roundworms are round, whitish and can be up to 10 cm (4 in) long. They have a direct developmental cycle without an intermediary host and are undoubtedly one of the most common intestinal parasites. Infection is caused as a result of the cat absorbing worm eggs in food, or by licking other worm-infested cats. Infected play areas and general lack of hygiene very quickly cause worm infestation. Kittens get infected by worm eggs in the coat and around the nipples of their mother. For this reason worming is strongly recommended for pregnant animals. Severe attacks can produce catarrh-like inflammations of the small intestine, causing severe diarrhoea. Kittens are particularly susceptible. Symptoms are loss of appetite, which alternates with voracious feeding, extreme thirst, dribbling, vomiting, wind and diarrhoea. The coat becomes dull, and there is a visible weight loss. It is not uncommon for pneumonia to set in, as a result

of the larvae spreading to the lungs. Fear, nervousness, stereotyped twisting movements and cramps may occur. Utter exhaustion of the animal may lead to death.

Treatment with worming medicine prescribed by the veterinary surgeon should be given, and repeated after 14 days. Bed, covers, underlay and other objects used daily by the cat, should be burned, boiled for half an hour or be dry-cleaned, during which process the chemicals used will kill the eggs.

Tapeworms   Tapeworms are flat intestinal parasites made up of segments, requiring intermediary hosts for their development. Different types of tapeworms use a variety of hosts, such as rats, mice, hares, rabbits, fish, fleas, lice and human beings. Tapeworms occur mostly in adult cats. Mild attacks will usually cause increased appetite, but accompanied by a shaggy, lustreless coat and slight apathy. Now and again segments of tapeworms may be found in the coat around the anal region or may be passed in the stool. These segments resemble small grains of rice or rye or pumpkin seeds. More severe attacks produce diarrhoea, usually accompanied by varying appetite and vomiting, but both diarrhoea and constipation can occur. The animal soon begins to show signs of emaciation and gets cramps. Since exhaustion rapidly leads to death, the veterinary surgeon should be consulted without delay. Before any prescribed treatment is given, the animal should not be fed for 12 to 18 hours. Any other method of treatment is useless and ineffective.

Other endoparasites   Hookworms, which destroy the intestinal wall, are less common in cats. Symptoms of hookworm-infestation are diarrhoea, which may sometimes be blood-stained, anaemia and emaciation. Here too, death can occur as a result of general exhaustion. Kittens are particularly at risk. The treatment prescribed by the veterinary surgeon should be repeated after an interval of several days.

230

Coccidiae are microscopically small, single-celled organisms that belong to the family sporozoa. They produce enteritis with bloody diarrhoea, causing young kittens to die very quickly. But often repeated reinfection causes a long drawn-out illness. Cats tend to lose their appetite, and have heavy, blood-streaked diarrhoea. The mucous membranes become pale, the stomach becomes distended and very sensitive, the coat dull and lifeless. The animal becomes sleepy and apathetic and eventually dies from general exhaustion.

This illness is very easily mistaken for Feline Infectious Enteritis. Only the veterinary surgeon can deal with it.

The development of parasites on the host animal takes approximately ten days. Stools must be removed immediately and destroyed. All objects and accommodation in contact with the animal must be disinfected daily with a 2 per cent solution of sodium hydroxide in boiling water. The animals under treatment must be kept in isolation until their stools are free from parasites.

Trichinellae are hairworms that belong to the roundworm group. The cat can become infected by consuming meat contaminated with trichinae, or from mice or rats. Trichinosis is, however, extremely rare. Vomiting, diarrhoea, listlessness, loss of weight and stiffness of the limbs are the symptoms to watch for.

Liver flukes are trematoda, whose development is tied to snails as intermediary hosts, and to freshwater fish as secondary hosts. Their developmental process is highly complex. Liver fluke in cats is more common in certain countries, such as Italy, France, Holland, Sweden, Romania, the Soviet Union, China and Japan. Both the varieties that appear in cats can also occur in humans. The infection is caused as a result of eating raw fish. Its effects are inflammation of the bile duct and liver, which affects the digestion and causes vomiting and apathy.

External disorders The cat's skin is very sensitive, since its fur normally provides it with good, and reliable protection. For this reason cats should preferably not be bathed. The skin performs several functions that are vital to the entire organism. Statistically skin diseases come second highest among all cat ailments. They may have external or internal causes and the

Dragging its rear on the ground may be a sign that a cat has worms

symptoms are correspondingly variable, consequently a skin disease may be very difficult to diagnose.

Itching Itching is one indication of a skin disease. It is not necessarily accompanied by a visible alteration in the skin or by the appearance of parasites. It may be localised in certain areas but may also rapidly spread all over the skin The extent is easily recognised by whether the sick cat scratches determinedly at one particular area or whether it scratches indiscriminately all over. The cause may be an allergic reaction to some cleaning agent used in the home, to cosmetics or to other chemical agents. It could also be precipitated by some nervous disorder. Hormonal changes both in the female and in the tom could play some part in producing itching. One frequent cause is disturbance of the diet caused by incorrect or unbalanced feeding. In the case of one Siamese tom, sudden itching deteriorated over a period of several weeks to total hair loss, and raw, severely inflamed skin all over the body. The tom had been fed exclusively on liver and lung, since it allegedly refused to eat anything else. Only after an extremely long-drawn-out and difficult period of changing the cat's diet, did the unfortunate creature's condition gradually improve. Incorrect diet may, of course, also be the cause of deficiencies of vitamins, mineral salts and trace elements. However, the underlying causes of such apparently simple disorders are mostly very difficult to trace. It is essential to consult the veterinary surgeon.

Hair loss An obvious indication of skin disease is alopecia (hair loss). Here again, the cause is frequently linked with imbalance in the diet or with organic or infectious diseases. Sometimes the condition will cure itself within a very short space of time.

There is also a form of alopecia that is present at birth. It is rare, and is frequently limited to one small area on the body. Where this occurs, the kitten should not be allowed to live.

Matted hair will be felt when stroking the cat—especially in longhairs. It may sometimes be present all over the body. The cat cannot rid itself of this by its usual licking. This type of matting should be removed very carefully with scissors. However, the owner should do this only if he is absolutely certain that the matting is not caused by small skin ulcers.

Skin inflammation Causes of genuine skin inflammation accompanied by visible signs of disease, such as redness, swelling, itching, pustules and vesicles, scabby and crusty patches, moist lesions and hair loss constitute eczema. Apart from the causes of itching already mentioned, chief of which is an unbalanced diet, other possible causes may be worm-infestation, skin parasites, nephritis, poisoning or infectious illnesses. Even a continued lack of exercise or obesity may be responsible for eczema. Diagnosis is extremely difficult. Only the veterinary surgeon can help.

In order for treatment with medication to be successful, the affected area plus a 30 mm ($1\frac{1}{4}$ in) wide band of unaffected skin must be shaved. This enables light, air and sun—all essential healing factors—to act on the affected skin. Warm paraffin oil will soften scabs. The medication is usually specific to one particular form of eczema and no one treatment will cure every type of inflammation. Treatment of eczema is a long and complicated process. In order to prevent the cat from scratching or licking off the applied ointment 232 or other medication, it may be necessary to put a paper collar around its neck or to apply bandage bootees over its paws. A healthy adequate, nourishing and varied diet and appropriate care and handling of the animal are important factors in assisting the healing process.

Skin parasites   No matter how scrupulous and clean the cat is, it is impossible to prevent it from being attacked at some time by skin parasites of one kind or another. All the symptoms listed above, from straightforward itching to extensive eczema may occur in cats affected by external parasites.

Fleas, lice, ticks and mallophagae are easy to recognise, even when they occur in small numbers. They are comparatively simple to combat, and it is not usually necessary to consult the veterinary surgeon.

Without necessarily being visible, fleas or lice cause itching, increased restlessness in the cat, hair loss, and in protracted cases, signs of eczema. If the parasites proliferate extensively, especially on under-nourished and sick cats, the distress and deterioration suffered by the cat can cause emaciation, and even death.

The species of flea that may occur are cat flea, dog flea, and less commonly, the human flea. The eggs are laid not on the host animal, but in its bed and in cracks and joints in floorboards. Larvae develop from the eggs, which shed their skin several times before pupating into a cocoon.

Lice lay their eggs, or 'nits', directly on the skin of the host and attach them to the host's hair by a secretion. Individual fleas and lice can usually be found by inspecting the coat and killed. Otherwise, contact insecticides may be used, but not for kittens or nursing queens. The dusting powder (derris, pyrethrum or gammexane) is applied against the direction of the fur. Gammexane should not be left on so that the cat can lick it, the others may be left longer but since all are contact poisons which kill the flea the powder may be brushed out soon after the application is complete. In dealing with fleas, it is important not only to destroy the parasites on the animal but also to remove all the eggs. The cat's bed, covers and other accessories should all be boiled, dry-cleaned or burned. The treatment should be repeated after an interval of 10 to 14 days. The cat flea is, moreover, an intermediary host and a carrier of tapeworm.

The life cycle of ticks or wood-ticks is dependent on three hosts. The larva form, the chrysalid form and the fully-grown adult are found on grasses, shrubs and trees, and attach themselves to the fur of the cat, as it moves through the undergrowth. They are several millimetres long, greyish-brown and sack-like in appearance. They attach themselves to the host's skin and engorge themselves with its blood, which causes their bodies to inflate like balloons. This produces itching, swellings and inflammations in the affected cat. The utmost care must be exercised in the removal of these parasites. If they are pulled out by force, only the body of the tick will come away, and the head of it will be left buried in the cat's skin resulting in an infected sore. For this reason, it is always best to dab the tick with alcohol to anaesthetise it. After two or three minutes the parasites can be easily and satisfactorily removed in their entirety with tweezers.

Mange   Far more unpleasant is mange, which is caused by mites. Notoedres mange is the commonest and is produced by a mite that burrows its way under the skin, especially

233

of the head or neck. The mites are passed from animal to animal, or from contact with objects to which mites are attached. Sick, under-fed or ill-cared for cats, are most prone to attack. The mange almost always begins on the head, especially on the forehead, the outer ear and eyelids, it may then spread to the paws and the remainder of the body. The irritation causes intense scratching, licking and gnawing, and the cat rubs itself raw, producing eczema. The hair falls out and scabs and crusts form. The cat's constant scratching rapidly transmits the mange to other parts of the body. The effects are apathy, loss of appetite, anaemia, and in severe cases death. This mite also attacks humans, and causes the same skin irritation and scratching. They do not, however, propagate on a human host, and eventually die, provided there is no constantly renewed contact with infected cats. Combating these mites in cats is not easy and treatment is a lengthy process. The veterinary surgeon will prescribe applications of special contact insecticides. All the objects with which the cat comes into contact must be thoroughly cleaned and disinfected.

Demodex or acarus mange is comparatively rare in cats. It results in hair loss in the areas around the eyes, nose and ears, and produces visible inflammation and scaly patches.

The harvest mite attacks the cat in the late summer and autumn. It attacks the cat, as well as other mammals and birds, during its larval stage. The affected areas appear reddish-yellow, and are usually seen in those parts of the body where the skin is particularly soft such as between the toes, on the face and on the surface of the belly. Powder, shampoo (with gammexane) and aerosol spray treatments are available.

Otodectic or ear mange is very common and is caused by ear-mites, which are 0.5 mm in length. They live in the outer lining of the cat's ear, burrowing under the skin and feeding on the lymph that is discharged. The constant irritation causes inflammation and affected animals will persistently shake and scratch their heads. The inflamed auditory canal finally becomes blocked up with purulent wax full of mites. Malaise, weakness, loss of appetite, emaciation and in severe cases perforation of the ear-drum, are further consequences. Treatment should always be left to the veterinary surgeon. At the very outset, when buying a cat, the ears should be inspected to make sure they are clean and healthy.

However, inflammation of the ear is not always caused by mites. Excessive wax secretion, suppuration caused by draughts or as a result of water entering the cat's ear while bathing, as well as the presence of foreign bodies, such as plant seeds or splinters of any kind, can produce a very painful inflammation. The owner should not attempt to treat the animal himself.

Fungi Skin fungi or dermatomycosis are rarer, but also more dangerous, since most are obstinate in their response to treatment. Distinct types of fungi are *Trichophyton* and *Microsporum* or herpes tonsurans. The infection can be passed directly from animal to animal or indirectly via an intermediary host. Cross-infection to human beings easily occurs. In human beings dermatomycosis can follow a highly virulent course. The symptoms are not always clear, since there can be atypical manifestations and the process of inflammation and suppuration can often mask the true condition. It is not unusual for itching to be absent. Scaly, blistery and crusty patches form, and hair loss or breaking **234** off of hairs in circular patches occurs. There is an incubation period of from one to four weeks, between the contraction and appearance of the illness. Local or even complete clipping of the cat is necessary, since the affected hairs break off and cause reinfection. A good, healthy diet helps the sick cat through this lengthy illness. The treatment prescribed by the veterinary surgeon takes many weeks and requires the owner's utmost patience and care. It must be continued until all traces of hypha, which are visible under the microscope, have either completely disappeared or have all died off. Being cured from one attack of fungi does not give the cat immunity from future attacks. There is no vaccination against it. If there are several cats in a home, then the animals must all be treated, until they are all well again. Medication prescribed for this type of illness in humans must not be given to the cat.

Rickets Osteomalacia (rickets) is a deficiency disease, an avitaminosis. It results from deficiency of Vitamin D, which causes a disturbance in the metabolism of calcium and phosphorus. Adequate Vitamin D is essential for the normal development of bone. It is likewise essential for the absorption of calcium from the intestine, which would otherwise be excreted, unused. Vitamin D governs the entire calcium and phosphorus metabolism.

The symptoms of rickets are enlargement of the joints, lumps along the ribs and short, bowed front legs. Related to these symptoms are stiffness and obvious difficulty in movement. Irregular shedding of teeth may also occur. A healthy varied diet, fresh air and sunshine, vitamin supplements—especially Vitamin A and D preparations—or regular doses of cod-liver oil will prevent rickets from developing. Regular vitamin or cod-liver oil supplements are indispensable, particularly for pregnant or nursing queens.

Poisoning Symptoms of poisoning will occur in cats from time to time, as a result of their having eaten any one of a great variety of injurious substances. Diagnosis is extremely difficult, unless you see the poison consumed and know the antidote. The effects could be lethal and the animal should be taken to the veterinary surgeon with all possible speed, since he alone may be able to save it. He will attempt to remove the poison from the cat's body by pumping out its stomach, making it vomit, and inserting an enema. However, none of these measures will be effective after four hours have elapsed. The symptoms are difficult to differentiate and could frequently be confused with many other illnesses. Often there is no rise in temperature; on the contrary, poisoning usually produces a drop in temperature. However, any part of the animal, such as the skin, mucous membranes, respiratory organs, digestive tract or nervous system, may show general symptoms of illness.

Pesticide poisoning The most likely form of poisoning is from rat or mouse poison, which has been absorbed either directly by the cat or indirectly via poisoned prey caught and eaten by the cat. It is worth mentioning here that rat bites, too, can be highly dangerous. The bites easily develop into ugly abscesses. The area surrounding the wound should immediately be freed of hair, and bathed twice daily in hydrogen peroxide. If the bite becomes inflamed or the surrounding area swells up, then the animal should be taken immediately to the veterinary surgeon.

Pesticides, weed-killers and fertilisers may contain arsenic and phosphorus. Acute arsenic poisoning produces severe vomiting, salivation, intense thirst and cardiac weakness accompanied by trembling and paralysis. Touching the cat's body will evoke intense cries of pain. Chronic arsenic poisoning produces bloody, evil-smelling diarrhoea, unsteadiness, weakness and greenstick fractures of the back limbs, refusal to eat, staggering, skin inflammations, emaciation and a subnormal temperature.

Phosphorus poisoning will produce the same symptoms. As a rule, however, the course of the illness is very acute (that is to say the poison acts more quickly than does arsenic). The mucous membranes may become inflamed, blood-stained urine and even skin bleeding may occur, and the cat's breath and vomit smell distinctly of garlic. Weakness, severe cramps and coma, will rapidly lead to the death of the animal. As in the case of arsenic poisoning, milk, oil and fats should be withheld at all costs.

Strychnine poisoning produces convulsions. This is why the most striking symptoms, apart from salivation, vomiting, state of anxiety and hyperexcitability, are tetanic spasms. These spasms are triggered off by the slightest stimulus, such as a touch, noise or light and extend throughout the animal's whole body. Respiratory cramps are soon followed by the death of the animal through asphyxiation.

Effective rat poisons are Warfarin compounds, which suppress the activity of Vitamin K, and prevent the production of prothrombin, leading to internal bleeding in rats. The cat is susceptible to quite small quantities of this poison and eating a rat or mouse that has ingested only a minimal amount, but has been affected enough to make it easy to catch, can be fatal.

Poisoning by contact insecticides   Poisoning can easily occur from the contact insecticides used to combat skin parasites on the cat if the drug is used carelessly or in dosages that are too high. Enclosing the cat in a linen bag is advisable. Symptoms such as trembling, loss of balance, acute fear, sudden running and jumping, and convulsions are the result of serious damage to the central nervous system. Death can occur after one to two hours but often only after one or two days. In treatment the first step is to remove immediately any pesticide powder that still remains in the coat. Milk, oils and fat should never be used as emetics or laxatives.

Nicotine can also produce poisoning in a cat, for example if the cat eats bits of a cigarette. Death in this case is caused by respiratory paralysis. Excessive doses of worming agents can also produce toxic effects, such as vomiting, diarrhoea, epileptic-type convulsions and irregular breathing. Products used in technological processes can also cause poisoning in house and pedigree cats. The chemicals which are most likely to be encountered are carbolic acid, and related substances such as cresol, creolin, creosote, naphthol, carbol, tar oils and naphthalene. These substances are commonly found in ointments for skin diseases, in disinfectants, pesticides, wood preservatives and in tar and asphalt products. No agent containing phenol should be used in a home where a cat is kept. The poisons can enter the cat's body not only as a result of its licking its fur or licking objects that have been contaminated, but also can be absorbed through the skin. Treatment is usually hopeless, and death cannot be prevented. Insect stings from bees, wasps and hornets will occasionally produce signs of poisoning. The symptoms that occur in such cases are restlessness, licking, writhing on the ground, swellings and respiratory distress. Even swallowing insects, such as grasshoppers, for example, and nibbling poisonous plants—many indoor plants are poisonous—can have toxic effects on the cat.

The many possible ways in which poisoning can occur, and the difficulty in differentiating between the symptoms shows how important it is for the veterinary surgeon treating the animal to be given all the relevant information. Only if the animal is brought to the veterinary surgeon immediately after having absorbed the poison, is there any chance of saving the animal.

Panleukopenia or Feline Infectious Enteritis

Panleukopenia is an inflammation of the pharyngeal space and the gastro-intestinal canal that predominantly attacks kittens and young cats up to the age of two years. The infection is most likely to be contracted in catteries, in animal clinics, at cat shows and in homes where the infection is already present.

Symptoms The symptoms are not always typical. Often only an experienced and very observant owner will spot the first signs of this kind of illness. A slight rise in temperature, loss of appetite and listlessness, and a tendency to seek out cool and moist places to lie in, are indications. The picture rapidly deteriorates: the temperature soars to 41°C (105°F); the inflammation of the gastro-intestinal tract causes persistent vomiting of frothy, yellowy-green mucus; and the cat refuses all food. It will place its paws or head in the water bowl, or sometimes even sit right over it. It gives loud cries of pain and its skin and tissue become wrinkled and as dry as parchment. The animal is utterly exhausted and rapidly becomes emaciated. At this state as a rule it can no longer stand. Its eyelids become gummed up and the eyes sink deep into their sockets; the coat becomes drab and unkempt. There follows a dramatic drop in temperature to below 35°C (95°F). If the illness follows a rapid course, the cat may die within 24 hours, but it may not die for about five days. There is a very high mortality rate of 80–90 per cent.

It is advisable to disinfect all infected areas with the utmost thoroughness, and to burn all objects the cat has used, such as covers, pillows, bed, etc. A strong, well-fed cat that is protected from draughts stands a better chance in such an illness, and consequently kittens should never be taken away from their mother too early. (In our experience, the best age is between nine and ten weeks.) The veterinary surgeon's instructions must be strictly followed. Even when the acute signs of illness are abating, the cat will probably still need to be fed by hand, and given an invalid diet. A solution of glucose in water, Lactol, Complan and other such predigested invalid foods, high protein baby foods and meat essences are all suitable and liver should be included in the diet.

Protection Vaccination at the right time provides fairly reliable protection against this illness. It is obligatory for cats that are going to be left in a cattery or exhibited in a show. This vaccination is given for the first time at the age of three months. Kittens tolerate the vaccination without any complication whatsoever. Some people believe that worming the animal prior to vaccination may help achieve immunity. A choice of vaccine exists. The most recent requires one shot which, it is claimed, gives immunity within 48 hours. With the other method two vaccinations are given at an interval of 14 days. Immunity comes into effect some 10 to 14 days after the vaccination. Booster doses need to be given

237

annually. Vaccination for the first time can also be carried out on older animals, practically at any age. Keep the certificate the veterinary surgeon will issue as proof of immunisation, should you require it for a boarding cattery or to show a stud owner, and as a reminder of when the booster is due.

Virus influenza   A second virus disease, which affects the cat's respiratory tract, is virus influenza, which comes in two forms although the symptoms and treatment are similar for both forms. It is frequently accompanied by leukopenia. The mucous membranes of the nose, the pharynx, the larynx and the trachea become inflamed. Nasal discharge, sneezing, coughing, purulent discharge from the eyes, gummed-up eyelids, difficulty in swallowing and loss of appetite are further symptoms. The cat develops a fever, and the inflammation may spread to the bronchi and lungs. The illness generally lasts for 14 days, after which time the cat's condition gradually improves. The mortality rate is comparatively low if treatment is started in time. Oriental cats and kittens under one year old seem most susceptible to the disease.

Rabies is one of the most dangerous of infectious diseases, and can be transmitted from the animal to man. It is caused by a virus that can produce a disease of the central nervous system in all mammals. Although rigorous quarantine restrictions have so far kept it out of Great Britain, the disease is distributed world-wide, and in recent decades it has been on the increase in Central Europe. The chief source of infection is the local wildlife such as fox, badger and marten, but deer and fallow deer have often been found to be suffering from it. **Rabies**

Transmission   The animal that most commonly transmits the disease to humans is the dog. However, because it is far more difficult to restrain cats from roaming in fields and woods than it is to restrain dogs, cats contract the disease far more frequently, usually as a result of bites sustained in fights with foxes. Anyone permitting a cat to run loose in an area where rabies is prevalent is acting irresponsibly. Entry to some continental European countries is dependent on evidence that the animal in question has been vaccinated against rabies no later than four weeks before the date of entry. Such vaccination is considered effective for 11 months.

Transmission of the disease usually occurs as a result of bites or scratches, but can also result from contamination of wounds already present on the skin or via intact mucous membranes, since the virus is present in the saliva and blood of the sick animal. Rabies is invariably fatal in cats. The incubation period, from the time of infection to the appearance of the first symptom of the disease, is highly variable, since it depends on many different factors. As a rule it is between two and four weeks, but can take longer, even up to eight weeks. The infection can be passed on to other animals and to man during the incubation period.

Course of the illness   There are three stages, the preliminary stage, the stage of excitation and the paralytic stage. The symptoms are frequently atypical, making it difficult to diagnose the disease in good time.

Initially, the most striking symptoms are a complete change in the behaviour of the cat. In the first stage the animals are very timid and tend to hide, but they will also **238** become extremely affectionate, which can change quite suddenly to biting or scratching. This is particularly dangerous. Often the animals miaow continuously, and may sound hoarse. Some cats will devour non-edible objects, such as wood, stones, earth or other unsuitable substances. Increased salivation becomes evident, and food and water are refused. The appearance of the pupils changes, and they may be of unequal size. The cat has a constant urge to hide; some crawl away and remain in hiding until they die. For this reason utmost care must be taken with animals that are found dead. The preliminary stage lasts from half a day to three days, and leads on to the stage of frenzy.

Skeleton of a house cat

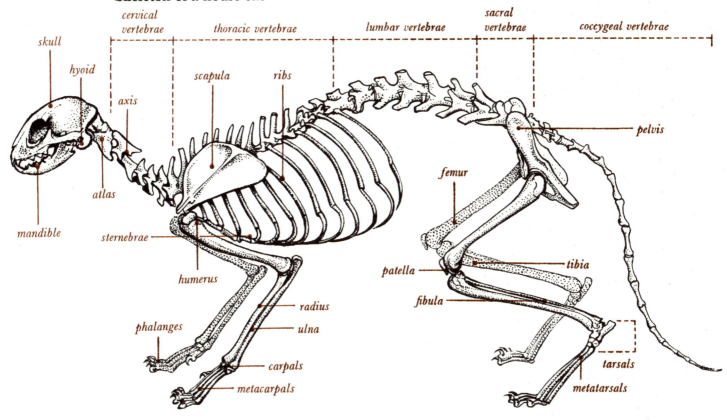

During the stage of excitation the cat runs about quite aimlessly and may cover considerable distances. Everything that happens to cross its path is attacked, bitten and scratched. The cat loses its customary timidity even towards dogs, other large animals or humans, and will attack them, too. Since cats usually tend to spring up at humans, injuries often occur on the head, which is particularly dangerous. Offering them food or water unleashes fits of rage. The cat displays signs of paralysis on one side of its face and the paralysis then extends to its limbs. Between one and three days later the stage of paralysis and depression sets in. Altogether rabies normally takes from three to six days but it can take longer before the agonising death occurs. The disease may last for more than one month, in which case it takes a highly atypical form. Many of the characteristic symptoms are completely absent, for example the tearing about, the raging and the biting. **239** Instead the symptoms of paralysis rapidly advance. This form is known as 'dumb rabies'.

Treatment of cats for rabies is pointless and the animal must be captured and allowed to die. Then a laboratory must inspect its brain to confirm that it had rabies—this is apparent only from brain changes that take place shortly before death. The veterinary surgeon, public health commissioner and police immediately set all the essential procedures into motion. The suspected animal must be taken into safe keeping and not be touched. Once a case of rabies has been confirmed the area is immediately declared a prohibited area for cats, and all stray cats are shot. People who have had contact with animals suspected of being rabid or who have been bitten or scratched, must immediately go for medical treatment with anti-rabies serum.

As there is no cure for rabies in animals, and as throughout the world some 3,000 to 6,000 animals die an agonising death every year as a result of this disease, these harsh measures are fully justified.

The domestic cat has a normal life expectancy of between 10 and 14 years, but in exceptional cases it may live as long as 17 and even 20 years. Indeed, there are a few instances, where pet cats have lived considerably longer. There is the case of the British cat called 'Ma', who had reached the unlikely age of 35 when it was put to sleep. The only question we would ask is, whether it is in fact always to the animal's advantage to live to a record age.

Senility and
hereditary diseases

Manifestations of ageing One possible condition in elderly cats is toothache—though this can, of course, occur at any age. Decay, loosening and loss of teeth and gum disease are not uncommon. The usual signs are painful chewing, increased salivation, gradual loss of weight, refusal of food and, in complicated cases, spasms of the jaws. Extraction of the affected teeth will usually produce rapid relief.

A far more serious condition, mainly found in old age, is inflammation of the kidneys, or nephritis. The symptoms begin with intense thirst and increased output of urine. The cat may even lap up water spilled on the floor or dirty puddles to quench its thirst. Loss of appetite, emaciation and apathy follow. In severe cases this leads to uraemia. Treatment is seldom successful.

Retention of urine, where the cat repeatedly tries to pass urine without success, is most common in ageing castrated toms but can also occur in other conditions. For example, it can be due to a nervous disorder, resulting from the paralysis of certain spinal nerves, or it can result from a blockage of the urethra by substances precipitated out of the urine. These cases can be treated by the veterinary surgeon. A clearly perceptible loss of weight and chronic irregularities in digestion, accompanied by loss of appetite and apathy, are indications of cirrhosis of the liver. The chances of successful treatment are poor.

Older, overfed cats, or cats that have been fed on too rich a diet, may develop paralysis or dragging of the back legs. This condition may appear by the age of eight years. The veterinary surgeon will prescribe a course of vitamins and an appropriate diet.

Signs of ageing are most noticeable in the coat. The face becomes distinctly greyer, the coat is frequently less well groomed, or may even be neglected completely, and gradually loses its colour. The sensory function of the eye, the ear and the nose become less acute, and the cat spends more and more time resting.

240

The breed numbers are those used by the Governing Council of the Cat Fancy and the Fédération Internationale Féline Européenne.

Long-haired cats (Persian cats)

In the following breeds the head is round and broad with small ears spaced well apart, a broad muzzle, a short nose and full cheeks. The body is cobby and massive, without being coarse, and stands on short, strong legs. The animal has a well-balanced form. The tail is short and bushy. The coat is long and silky, with a full frill.

1 Black

The coat should be raven black with no trace of rustiness, white hairs or markings of any kind. Kittens often have a very grey or rust-coloured coat but, as they grow up, this will usually turn deep black. Eyes are copper coloured or deep orange and must not have a green rim.

2 Blue-eyed white

The coat should be pure white with no trace of any other colour. The eyes should be a deep, pure blue.
Kittens often have grey or black patches on the head which usually disappear as they grow older. Such patches are frequently a sign that the cat will not suffer from the deafness associated with blue-eyed white cats.

2a Orange-eyed white

Identical to the Blue-eyed white except for the eye colour which should be orange or deep copper. These cats do *not* carry the deafness factor.

2b Odd-eyed white

Identical to the two preceding varieties except for the eye colour. One eye should be orange or deep copper, the other deep blue.

3 Blue

The coat may be any shade of blue provided that the colour is pure and even. The ears should be well-tufted. The eyes should be a deep orange or copper with no trace of green.

4 Red-self

The coat should be a deep, rich red without stripes, patches or other markings. The ears should be well-tufted. The eyes should be deep copper in colour.

5 Cream

The coat should be absolutely pure cream, pale to medium in strength and even in tone without any shading or markings. The eyes should be deep copper in colour.

6 Smoke

The contrasting coat should be black on the body, shading to silver on the sides and flanks. The head and feet should be black, the extra long frill and ear tufts should be silver. The undercoat should be as near white as possible. Eyes are orange or copper.

6a Blue smoke

This variety is identical to the preceding Smoke except that those parts of the coat which are black in the Smoke are blue in the Blue smoke. Eyes are orange or copper.

7 Silver tabby

The coat should be a pure, pale silver with jet black markings. Any hint of brown is counted as a fault. The cheeks should be marked with two or three spirals and two collar-like rings, set close together, should cross the chest. There should be butterfly markings on the shoulders, black stripes on the front paws, deep bands running down the saddle and sides and regular rings around the tail. The eyes may be green or hazel.

8 Brown tabby

The coat should be a rich tawny sable with black markings as described for the Silver tabby. The eyes can be hazel or copper in colour.

9 Red tabby

The coat should be a deep, rich red with the markings, as described for the preceding varieties, clearly defined. The eyes should be deep copper in colour.

10 Chinchilla

The undercoat should be pure white and the coat on the back, flanks, head and tail tipped with black. This tipping should be evenly distributed to give a sparkling silver appearance. The chin, ear tufts, stomach and chest should be pure white. The nose tip is brick-red, the lips, paw pads and the edges of the eyelids are black. The eyes should be emerald or blue-green in colour.

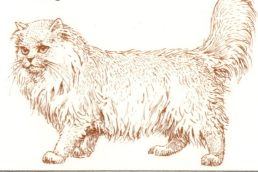

11 Tortoiseshell

The coat is made up of three colours: black, red and cream which should be clearly differentiated in patches over both the body and the face. The eyes should be deep orange or copper.

242

Longhairs

12 Tortoiseshell and white
The tri-colour coat of the tortoiseshell should be evenly distributed and broken and interspersed with patches of white. The eyes should be deep orange or copper.

12a Bi-colour
The coat may be white patched with any other single solid colour with the patches evenly distributed and neither more than two-thirds coloured nor more than half white. The face should be patched with both. Eyes should be orange or copper.

13 Blue-cream
In Europe and Britain the coat should be a softly intermingled mixture of blue and cream. In North America the two colours should be separated into clearly defined patches. Eyes should be deep copper or orange.

13b Colourpoint (Himalayan)
The coat should be long, thick and soft in texture with a full frill and colour and markings as described for varieties 24 and 32, Siamese. All the Siamese colours and patterns are recognised in Britain except for the Tabby-point. Eyes should be a clear, bright blue. Some European bodies recognise only the Seal, Blue and Chocolate.

Birman
Long and low in the body with short legs and a long bushy tail, this animal has a wide, rounded head with full cheeks. The long, silky coat should have a full ruff and be wavy on the belly. Markings are like the points of the Siamese but the paws must be white with the white running up the back up the hind paws on the hock and ending evenly at the third joint of the front paws.

13c Seal point and Blue point
Although other colours have now been bred these are the only ones so far recognised for the Birman. The eyes of both should be bright blue.

Cameo
Recognised in America, but not in Britain or on the European continent, this is a white-coated cat with a tipping of red. There are three colour strengths: Shell, the palest, Shaded and Smoke (also known as Red Smoke). Eyes should be deep copper.

Peke-faced
Recognised only in America this is a variety coloured and patterned like either the Red-self or the Red tabby but with a brachycephalic face like that of the Pekinese dog.

Angora
Ancient Turkish breed, recognised in America. Small to medium in size with a smaller head than the Persian type, a longer nose, tapering face and longer ears. Its limbs are longer and it is finer boned. Only white cats currently recognised. Eyes may be blue, amber or odd-eyed.

Maine coon cat

Large and muscular breed, known only in America, more like the Angora body-type than the Persian. The fur is also shorter and lacks the full ruff of the usual longhair. Colour and pattern are not laid down but eyes should either match the coat as in other longhairs or be green.

Turkish cat

Similar to the Angora in conformation with the head a short wedge shape with a long nose and large, upright ears. The coat is long and silky with well tufted ears and toes. Not known in America.

13d Chalky white coat with auburn face with a white blaze and auburn rings around the tail. Eyes are light amber. Eye rims, nose tip, paw pads and inside the ears are pink.

Balinese

In conformation this is a Siamese cat but has long hair. It has been bred with Seal, Blue, Chocolate and Lilac points but is so far only recognised in America although being bred in England.

British short-haired cats

The British and European shorthair has a powerful body with a full broad chest, strong short legs with rounded paws, a short, thick tail with a rounded tip and a round head set on a short neck. The nose is short and straight, the ears small and rounded at the tips, the eyes large, round and wide open. The coat is short and dense.

14 **Blue-eyed white**
The coat should be pure white and the eyes deep sapphire blue.

14a **Orange-eyed white**
Identical to the Blue-eyed except for the eye colour which should be gold, orange or copper.

14b **Odd-eyed white**
Identical to the two preceding varieties except for the eye colours, one being blue the other orange.

15 **Black**
Coat should be jet black to the roots without any tinge of rust or sign of white hairs. Eyes are orange or copper in colour with no trace of green. Rusty tinge permissible in kittens.

16 **Blue**
Light to medium blue coat, even in colour with no shading, stripes or white patches. Eyes copper or orange (vivid green in Europe).

17 Cream
An even, warm cream, lighter shades preferred in Britain, for the coat. Eyes copper or orange in Britain, copper or hazel in Europe.

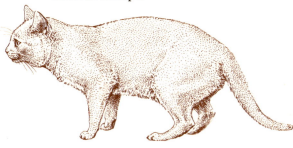

Tabby
The classic tabby pattern as in the long-haired descriptions has pencilling on the cheeks, an 'M' mark on the brow, a line from the corner of the eye, a vertical line down the back of the head to the butterfly-like shoulder markers, oyster-shaped blotches on the sides with surrounding rings, braceleted legs and ringed tail, the markings on each side of the body to be identical.

The mackerel tabby pattern, sometimes known as the tiger stripe has head, legs and tail as for the classic tabby. There should be an unbroken line along the spine from which narrow stripes run vertically down the body.

18 Silver tabby
The coat has deep black markings against a silver ground. Eyes may be green or hazel.

19 Red tabby
The markings are a deep red on a red ground, clearly differentiated. The eyes should be brilliant copper in Britain, orange or hazel in Europe.

20 Brown tabby
The markings are dense black on a coppery brown ground (or a warm sand colour in Europe). Eyes may be orange, hazel or deep yellow, and in Europe also green.

21 Tortoiseshell
The coat is black with clearly defined patches of red and cream evenly distributed. The eyes should be brilliant copper or orange, and in Europe also hazel.

22 Tortoiseshell and white
Black, cream and red patches should be equally balanced on white to make up the coat and the patchings should cover the head, cheeks, ears, back, tail and parts of the flanks. Eyes should be brilliant copper or orange, and in Europe may also be hazel.

28 Blue-cream
In Britain and Europe the two colours of the coat should be softly intermingled but in America they should form clearly defined patches. Eyes should be copper or orange.

30 Spotted
The head is marked like the classic tabby and the body and legs patterned with spots, as numerous and distinct as possible, with spots or broken rings on the tail desirable. Colour of the coat may be silver with black spots, brown with black, red with darker red or any other standard colour provided the spots are clearly contrasted. Eye colours follow those given for the basic coat colours.

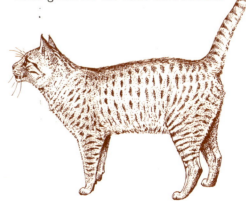

31 **Bi-colour** (Parti-colour)
Any solid colour and white provided that they be clearly patched and evenly distributed. Not more than two-thirds of the coat should be coloured or more than half white. The face should be patched and a white blaze is favoured. Eyes should be brilliant orange or copper, and may also be yellow in Europe.

36 **Smoke**
Grouped as the same variety in shorthairs the smoke may be black or blue with the colour-tipped hairs lying over a pale silver undercoat. Eyes may be yellow or orange.

Manx

The body is solid and compact with a very short back and rounded rump, deep flanks and unusually long hindlegs, which produce a hopping gait. There should be a definite hollow at the end of the spine. The head is large and round with prominent cheeks, the nose long but without a definite break, the ears larger than in the British shorthair and the eyes large and round. The coat is double with a thick undercoat.

25 The coat may be any of the colours accepted for British shorthairs and the eyes should be of appropriate colour for the coat.

Russian blue

This cat's long and graceful body is set on long legs with small oval feet. The head is a short wedge shape with a straight nose, prominent whisker pads, large, pointed ears and almond-shaped eyes set wide apart. The tail is fairly long and tapering. The coat is short, thick and very fine. Soft, silky, with a silvery sheen, it is double, and in texture like sealskin.

16a The coat should be a clear, even blue throughout. A medium shade is preferred in Britain, pale to lavender on the Continent. The eyes should be a vivid green.

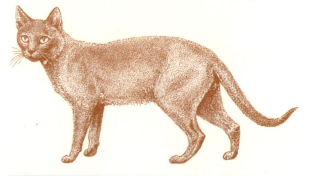

Abyssinian

A lithe cat of medium build, the medium length body has a fairly long, tapering tail. Feet are small and oval and the head broad and tapering to a firm wedge, set on an elegant neck. Ears are broad at the base, large and pointed and set well apart. Eyes large, well apart and in an oriental setting. The coat is short, fine and close-lying.

246

Shorthairs **23** **Usual**
Golden brown coat ticked with black, there being two or three bands of colour on each hair. Base hair ruddy orange or rich apricot. Belly and inside of legs harmonise with base hair. Tip of tail and back of hindlegs black. Eyes amber, hazel or green.

23a **Red**
Copper red coat, ticked with chocolate. Base hair deep apricot. Tip of tail and back of hindlegs chocolate. Eyes amber, hazel or green.

23b **Blue**
Provisionally recognised in Britain. Blue-grey coat ticked with deeper steel blue. Base hair pale cream or oatmeal. Tip of tail and back of hindlegs steel blue. Eyes amber, hazel or green.

Siamese
A medium-sized, long-bodied, svelte looking cat with a long tapering tail, slim legs (the hindlegs slightly longer than the front) with small oval feet. The head is long and wedge-shaped with a straight profile. The ears are large, pricked and wide at the base. The eyes are almond-shaped, set well apart and slope towards the nose. The coat is short and fine, thick, glossy and close-lying. A light-coloured coat is marked with darker 'points', characteristic of the breed, which comprise the paws, tail, ears, legs and face mask. The mask extends over the eyes and is extended by dark lines to link with the ears. In older cats the body colour will usually become darker on the back. In America some organisations recognise only the first four colour variations as Siamese, the others are known as Colorpoint shorthairs.

247

24 **Seal point**
Body colour of coat is cream, shading into pale warm fawn on the back. The points are a dark seal brown with no patching or brindling. Eyes are brilliant blue.

24a **Blue point**
Body colour is a glacial white, shading to blue on the back. The points are blue. The eyes are a vivid blue.

24b **Chocolate point**
The body colour is ivory all over. The points are a milk chocolate colour. The eyes are a vivid blue.

24c **Lilac point** (Frost-point)
The body colour is off-white shading, if at all, to tone with the points which are a pinkish grey. The eyes are vivid blue.

32 **Tabby point** (Lynx-point)
The body colour is pale and of the appropriate shade to match the colour of the points. The mask should consist of clearly defined stripes, as in the tabby. Legs and tail should be striped and ringed. The rest of the body should preferably be free of marking. The eyes should be a brilliant clear blue with the lids dark rimmed, or toning with the points.

Tortie tabby-points have tortoiseshell patching over the tabby pattern.

32a **Red point**
Body colour is white shading to apricot. Ears, mask and tail are bright reddish-gold, legs may be reddish-gold or apricot. Eyes are vivid blue.

32b **Tortie point**
Body colour is as in the equivalent solid colour Siamese but the points colour is mingled or patched with red and/or cream. Eyes are bright blue.

32c **Cream point**
As yet only provisionally recognised in Britain, this variety has a white body colour shading to palest cream with cream points and vivid blue eyes.

Burmese

A medium-sized, muscular cat with a strong, rounded chest, straight back and medium length tail tapering at the end to a rounded tip. The legs are slender, slightly longer at the back, and with small, oval feet. The head is rounded on the top with wide cheek bones and tapers to a short, blunt wedge. The ears are wide at the base and have rounded tips; their outer line continues the shape of the face. In Britain the eyes should be large and the upper line shows an oriental slant while the lower is rounded. American standards demand totally round eyes and rounded feet, whilst in Europe the eyes may be almond-shaped. The coat should be short, fine and close-lying with a particularly glossy sheen. In all colours the underparts may be lighter than the back.

27 **Brown**
The coat is a rich seal brown, with ears and mask slightly darker. Eyes may be any shade of yellow from chartreuse to amber but gold is preferred.

27a **Blue**
The coat is a soft, silver-grey. Eyes should be yellow but in Europe a greenish tinge is permitted.

27b **Chocolate**
The overall colour is a warm milk chocolate but slightly darker ears and mask are permitted. Eyes are yellow.

27c **Lilac**
The coat should be a pale dove-grey with a slight pinkish tinge. Eyes yellow.

27d **Red**
The coat should be a light tangerine. Slight tabby markings will be acceptable on the face (but not sides and belly) of an otherwise perfect cat. Ears are darker than the back. Eyes are yellow.

27e **Brown tortie**
A coat that is a mixture of brown and red has been provisionally recognised.

27f **Cream**
Coat colour should be a rich cream, slight tabby markings may be tolerated as in the Red (27d). Eyes yellow.

27g h j Blue tortie (Blue-cream), Chocolate tortie and Lilac tortie coats have all been provisionally recognised.

Shorthairs

Havana

Lithe and fine-boned, the Havana is in Britain and Europe of Foreign type and of the same conformation as the Siamese. In America a less extreme look is expected with oval eyes and rounded ear tips. The coat is short and glossy.

29 Coat colour is rich chestnut brown. The eyes should be green.

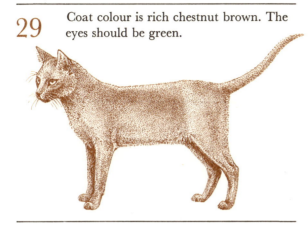

Foreign shorthairs (Oriental shorthairs)

These cats are, like the British Havana, self-coloured Siamese, except that some American standards ask for a slightly heavier cat.

29c
(29b in FIFE)
Lilac Coat colour should be a frosty-grey with a distinct pinkish tinge. The eyes should be green.

37
(FIFE 29sb)
Black (Ebony) Coat colour should be a deep, even black. The eyes should be green.

35 **White** The coat should be completely white. In Britain the eyes should be a brilliant blue but in Europe may also be gold.

Rex (Cornish Rex)

The coat is short, thick and plushy without guard hairs, and curls or waves, particularly on the back and tail. The head is wedge-shaped and the skull flat with a straight profile from forehead to tip of nose. Eyes are oval and medium in size. Ears are large, set high and widely based with rounded tips. The firm, muscular body is slender and of medium length with a long, thin, tapering tail and long legs with small, oval feet.

33 All colour variations are permitted but the eye colour should conform with that generally accepted for the coat.

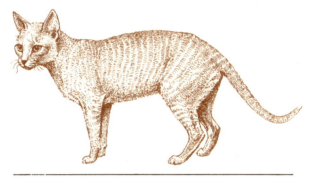

Rex (Devon Rex)

The coat is short, fine, soft and wavy, without guard hairs and with crinkled whiskers and eyebrows. The wedge-shaped head has full cheeks, a short muzzle and a strong chin with a distinct stop. The forehead curves back to a flat skull. The large eyes are oval and wide-set. The ears large, low set, wide-based and tapering to rounded tops, are covered with fine fur. The firm, muscular body has a broad chest, long legs and a long tail.

249

33a Coat may be in all colour variations. Eyes should match coat colour or, except in Siamese Rex, be chartreuse, green or yellow.

Korat

Medium-sized and muscular, this cat has a curved line to the back, a tail of medium length with a rounded tip and a heart-shaped face with a large, flat forehead and well-spaced, large eyes which are round when fully open but have an Asian slant when closed. It has a single coat which is short to medium in length.

34 Coat should be silver-blue all over, tipped with silver, the tipping not developing its full intensity until the cat is about two years old. Eyes should be brilliant green but kittens may have yellow eyes and an amber tinge is permitted.

American shorthair
(Domestic shorthair)

This solely American breed is a sturdy cat set on firm-boned legs which are longer than in the European shorthair. It has a longer nose but the muzzle is more square and the chin firm. The ears have slightly rounded tips and the large eyes have a slight slant to the outer edge. It is recognized in a wider range of colours than the European shorthair including Black smoke, Blue smoke, Chinchilla, Shaded silver, Cream tabby and Blue tabby.

Further Reading

Aberconway, C. *Dictionary of Cat Lovers* (Michael Joseph, 1968)

Artley, Alexandra. *The Great All-Picture Cat Show* (Astragal Books, 1977)

Beadle, Muriel. *The Cat: History, Biology and Behaviour* (Harvill Press, 1977)

Burton, R. *The Cat Family* (Macmillan Educational, 1976)

Eliot, T. S. *Old Possum's Book of Practical Cats* (Faber and Faber, 1975)

Epton, N. *Cat Manners and Mysteries* (Michael Joseph, 1975)

Fox, M. W. *Understanding Your Cat* (Bantam, 1977)

Gallico, Paul. *Honorable Cat* (Heinemann, nd)

Gay, John. *John Gay's Book of Cats* (David & Charles, 1975)

Harvey, Alan. *Knowing Cats. An Anthology for Unsentimental Cat-Lovers* (David & Charles, 1977)

Jude, A. C. *Cat Genetics* (TFH Publications, 1955)

Lauder, Phyllis. *The Batsford Book of the Siamese Cat* (Batsford, 1974)

—. *The Rex Cat* (David & Charles, 1974)

Lee, Elizabeth (Ed). *A Quorum of Cats* (Paul Elek, 1976)

Loxton, Howard. *Caring for your Cat* (David & Charles, 1975)

Loxton Howard and Warner, Peter. *Guide to the Cats of the World* (Elsevier/ Phaidon, 1975)

Macbeth, George and Booth, Martin, *The Book of Cats* (Secker and Warburg, 1976)

Manolson, F. *Language of your Cat* (Marshall Cavendish, 1977)

McCoy, J. J. *Complete Book of Cat Health and Care* (Teach Yourself Books, 1978)

McGinnis, Terri. *The Well Cat Book* (Wildwood House, 1976)

Necker, Claire. *The Cat's Got Our Tongue* (Scarecrow Press, 1973)

—. *The Natural History of Cats* (A. S. Barnes, New York, 1971)

Owen, Wendy. *Cat Lover* (P. Owen, 1976)

Pond, Grace (Ed). *Complete Cat Encyclopedia* (Heinemann, 1972)

—. *Cats and Kittens* (Batsford, 1976)

Pond, G. and Calder, M. *Longhaired Cat* (Batsford, 1974)

Pond, G. and Sayer, A. *Intelligent Cat* (Davis-Poynter, 1977)

Richards, Dorothy. *Handbook of Pedigree Cat Breeding* (Batsford, 1977)

Schneck, Stephen and Norris, N. *A to Z of Cat Care* (Collins, 1975)

Shaw, Richard. *The Cat Book* (Kaye & Ward, 1974)

Sillar, Frank Cameron and Meyler, Ruth. *Cats Ancient and Modern* (White Lion, 1976)

Study of the Cat (W. B. Saunders, 1977)

Tenent, Rose. *Pan Book of Cats* (Pan, 1976)

Wilson, Meredith. *Showing Your Cat* (Yoseloff, 1975)

—. *Cat Breeding and Showing: A Guide for the Novice* (A. S. Barnes, New York, 1973)

Acknowledgements

We should like to thank the following persons and institutions for kindly placing illustrations at our disposal:

Bürger, Magdeburg, P. 193 – Nos. 147, 148; P. 195 – No. 153

Josef-Hegenbarth-Archiv, Dresden, P. 6, 26, 86, 110, 180, 212

Manthey, Berlin-Bohnsdorf, P. 24 – Nos. 12, 13

Museum Rietberg, Zürich, P. 33 – No. 14; P. 35 – No. 17

Okapia, Frankfurt on Main, P. 34 – No. 16

Toepfer, Magdeburg, P. 22 – Nos. 8–10; P. 34 – No. 15

Vogel, Leipzig, P. 221 – Nos. 177, 178; P. 222 – Nos. 179, 180; P. 223 – Nos. 181, 182; P. 224 – Nos. 183, 184

Sources of Poems

P. 7 The Naming of Cats by T. S. Eliot,

P. 53 The Rum Tum Tugger by T. S. Eliot both from *Old Possum's Book of Practical Cats* (Faber & Faber Limited, London)

P. 87 The Bird Fancier by James Kirkup, from *Refusal To Conform* (Oxford University Press, London)

P. 90 Matthias and Atossa by Matthew Arnold, from *Cats, Cats, Cats* (Paul Hamlyn)

P. 111 To My Cat Jeoffrey by Christopher Smart 1722–1771, from *Jubilate Agno* (Rejoice in the Lamb)

P. 157 The Fireside Sphinx by Graham R. Tomson, from *Cats, Cats, Cats* (Paul Hamlyn)

P. 181 The Song of the Jellicles by T. S. Eliot, from *Old Possum's Book of Practical Cats* (Faber & Faber Limited, London)

P. 210 To a Cat by Algernon Charles Swinburne, from *Swinburne's Collected Poetical Works* (William Heinemann Ltd., London)

P. 213 The Old Woman and Her Cats by John Gay, from *John Gay Fables*

Index

Numbers in *italics* refer
to illustration numbers